Sardinia Baby!

First Printing 2015

Published by Rogue University Press

info@sardiniababy.com

ISBN-13: 978-1482776812

For Manu and Amelie

MENÚ DI RICETTE

Sardine al forno alla sarda
Sardinian oven baked sardines 5

Il Toast
Toast 7

Spaghetti al nero di seppia
Spaghetti with squid ink 21

Gnocchetti Sardi
Sardinian Gnocchetti 28

Olio piccante
Spicy oil 32

Porcetto arrosto
Roast suckling pig 40

Brasato di agnellone al finocchietto selvatico
Lamb with wild fennel 46

Panadas
Small meat & vegetable filled pies 50

Gamberi alla Vernaccia
King prawns with Vernaccia 63

Spaghetti ai frutti di mare al cartoccio
Seafood spaghetti baked in foil 76

Orata al forno
Oven baked bream 87

Ravioli di cinghiale con sugo di noci
Wild boar ravioli with walnut sauce 104

Zuppa Gallurese
Pecorino, focaccia & lamb broth bake 107

Spaghetti ai ricci di mare
Spaghetti with sea urchins 119

Biancomangiare
Sweet white pudding 123

Culurgiones
Potato, cheese & mint filled pasta from Nuoro 145

Zuppa di aragosta alla Castellanese con crostini di pane casareccio
Castelsardo lobster soup with crusty croutons 153

Tonno all'algherese
Tuna Algherese 166

Zucchine ripiene
Stuffed courgettes 174

Seadas
Large ravioli with ricotta and honey 181

Pardulas
Sweet ricotta cheesecakes 200

Agnello Sardo allo zafferano
Sardinian lamb with saffron 203

Manu's risotto
Risotto with saffron & sausage 213

Fregola con carne di capra
Fregola with goat 219

Ravioli di Nonna Peppa
Nonna Peppa's ravioli 225

Melanzane alla sassarese
Aubergines Sassarese 235

Limoncello 239

***

ACKNOWLEDGEMENTS

Grazie to all the wonderful people of Sardinia, especially Sassari. Without their inspiration and support this book would never have been possible. And a big thank you to all the people in the UK and beyond who believed in this project...you know who you are.

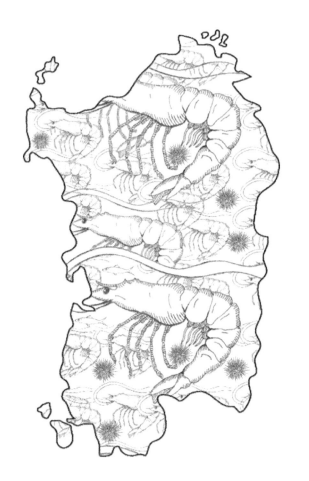

CHAPTER ONE

13th January 2009. I'm sitting in a bar called Gustaviños on the corner of Via Turritana and Via Eleonora D'Arborea in the medieval town of Sassari on the Italian island of Sardinia. I'm sipping a cold Ichnusa beer and in walks my old friend and one time colleague Tommaso Sommo. Tommaso owns the antique shop on the opposite corner and has a passion for theatre producing, or at least did. He orders a beer and we enjoy a comfortable silence.

My first trip to the island was back in 1991 when I toured the coast in an old white Fiat Panda on a camping holiday with my ex-girlfriend, Paola. We had just finished two gruelling years at the drama school École Jacques Lecoq in Paris so the month long stint in Sardinia was a much needed break. What I remember about the holiday and what most people associate with the island are its spectacular beaches but now having multiplied my initial visit by 72 months I can honestly say that there is more to this ancient paradise than just sand. And, contrary to popular belief, Sardines do not come from just Sardinia but they do know how to cook them.

SARDINE

Sardine al forno alla Sarda

Serves 2

Ingredients

- *500g fresh sardines*
- *300g ripe but firm tomatoes*
- *1 clove of garlic*
- *4-5 basil leaves*
- *small bunch fresh flat-leaf parsley*
- *1 small lemon*
- *2 tbls extra virgin olive oil*
- *salt*
- *pepper*

Preparation

Fillet sardines. Remove the heads and innards and discard. Scale and bone the fish then wash them under cold running water. Pat dry fillets with kitchen paper and put them aside.

Chop the parsley, garlic and basil. Squeeze lemon juice into a bowl. Peel the tomatoes, remove their seeds and chop their flesh. Preheat oven to 190 degrees. Add the olive oil, chopped herbs and tomatoes to the bowl. Season to taste with salt and stir.

Line a baking tray with greaseproof paper. Arrange the sardine fillets in a single layer and spoon over the chopped tomato mixture. Bake for about half an hour. If you see any cooking juice left during last minutes, increase temperature and bake for other 5 minutes.

***

I look at Tommaso and order a couple more beers. '*Auguri*' – congratulations he says.

It's 2003 and I'm working as a theatre director in the northern Italian town of Padova (approximately 30km from Venice) and, not wanting to return to the UK, decide to completely change my life. I have been offered a job directing A Midsummer Night's Dream in Sardinia and take the opportunity to make a fresh start. I don't know if there will be enough work to sustain me on the island but if the worst comes to the worst I can always travel back to the UK and direct there every so often. My contacts in Britain are strong and with cheap flights with Ryanair from Sardinia to London commuting is a possibility.

It's September and I'm waiting to board a ferry at the Italian port of Genoa having driven my Fiat Punto with all my worldly possessions the 340km from Padova via the A3, E70 and finally the E25 from Milan. My destination - the Sardinian port of Porto Torres in the north west of the island.

After five hours driving in stifling heat (my car doesn't have air conditioning) I arrive in Genoa port late afternoon two hours early for the scheduled departure and decide to treat myself to a well-deserved cold Peroni and something to eat. After all, I have negotiated the Italian *autostrada* and held my own in Genoa's rush hour despite having abuse hurled at me in Genovese none of which I understood but deduced that most of it could be translated into four letter words. My Italian isn't bad, I can understand *vaffanculo*, but dialects and colloquialisms are a complete mystery to me and better answered with the old smile and nod tactic.

To my absolute horror the bar is shut for refurbishments and I'm pointed in the direction of a small hut with an umbrella outside a couple of hundred meters away across the tarmac. Can I make it without sticking to the asphalt? The thought of a cold beer banishes any doubts I might have and I make it to the hut with shoes intact. There is nothing in the world that beats a cold beer in 35 degrees of heat but plenty to see off the only continental snack on offer - *il toast*.

Il Toast

Serves 1

Ingredients

- *2 slices of dry white nondescript bread*

- *1 slice of processed cheese*
- *1 slice of processed ham*

Preparation:
Remove all plastic packaging.
Place contents beneath a pre-heated grill for 1 minute.
Serve with a napkin.

***

With my appetite satisfied I order another beer and head for the relative sanctuary of the *Fanta* umbrella to admire the view. Genova is a fantastic looking city located between the Ligurian Sea and the Apennine mountains. From the Gulf of Genoa the metropolis sprawls up the mountainside in a maze of tightly packed, staggered buildings all with breath taking views of the harbour. Hard to see the connection with its sister city Baltimore in the USA. Christopher Columbus was born in Genoa (did he discover Baltimore?). And the city shares the same flag as the St George Cross. Apparently in 1190 the English were granted the right to use the Genoan crossed flag to have their ships protected by the numerous pirate attacks in the Mediterranean and Black Sea. For the privilege the English monarch at the time paid Genoa's Doge an annual fee. I wonder if we are still paying? Note to myself: ask present monarch.

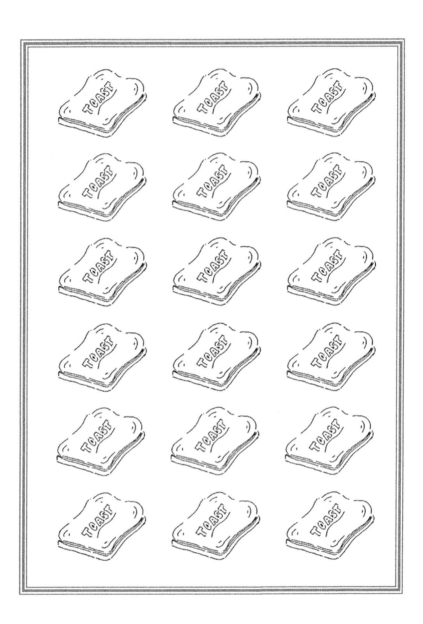

I always think of Genoa as the deep breath city, that last port of call on mainland Europe before embarking on a voyage into the unknown, throwing myself at the mercy of the Sardinians and a new life on a Mediterranean island. Melodrama aside I head for the Punto. The obligatory ruddy faced docker in fluorescent body warmer takes my ticket and points to the back of the car 'you better cover that lot up; you never know who's on these boats'. I have to admit that the sight of my flat screen TV poking out of my worldly possessions does look a bit tempting - but on a boat? I say 'fair play' to anyone who can steal a large television set from the boot of a car on a ferry in the middle of the Med then walk off with it without creating suspicion. I cover it up and drive on.

The Tirrenia ferry boat takes about ten hours and we eventually arrive at the north western port at seven in the morning. Situated 6km northwest of Monte d'Accoddi, Porto Torres is one of the island's oldest Roman towns and gateway to Sardinia serving Genoa, Marseilles, Barcelona, Civitavecchia and Toulon. Unfortunately there is very little visible evidence of the town's former Roman glory but instead an enormous oil refinery dominates the sky line. In contrast just 10km north of this industrial eyesore is Stintino with its fabulous beach La Pelosa. A truly magnificent feat of nature with soft white sand and clear blue waters to rival any beach in the world. And indeed The Times voted it among the top 50 beaches on the planet and that's a fuck of a lot of beaches. I descend to the car deck to check on the TV and prepare for 'disembarkation'. Despite being another hot day the sea is choppy and we have to wait before driving off. We are told that the ramp that connects the ferry to the dock won't stay in place making it impossible for a car to get across without plunging into the harbour. Great. Eventually after an hour's wait the fluorescent dockers decide that if the timing is right they can get one car off at time. At this point I'm wishing my Punto was the Lotus Elan that Roger Moor drives underwater in the Bond film The Spy Who Loved Me. Incidentally all those scenes were filmed in Sardinia on the Costa Smeralda. I'm jerked back to reality by fluorescent docker man waving and shouting '*Ajó. Ajó! Ajó!*' Presuming that to mean Go! Go! Go! as in Murray Walker and not 'don't whatever happens drive your car down that ramp' I gun the Punto into first, build up the revs, let the clutch out and fly off the boat. I make it. I congratulate myself on a near brush with death and consider having a well-deserved beer but remind myself that it's only 7.30 in the morning and I still have some driving to do.

My final destination and new home is the working town of Sassari about 10km south of Porto Torres and 30km west of Alghero. Sassari or Tàthari in Sardinian is the second largest city on the island after Cagliari in the south. With a population of approximately 170,000 it is roughly the same size as Peterborough but, in terms of climate, restaurants, medieval architecture and fine food completely different. Partly due to its turbulent past Sassari also boasts an impressive collection of art and cultural heritage sights. The city has been sacked more times than Mata Hari: in 1166 by the Genovese, in 1479 by the Spanish and again in 1527 by the French to name but a few. After 1861 Sassari became part of the new Kingdom of Italy and now has its very own flag which is more than can be said for some countries.

CHAPTER TWO

It's my first day of rehearsals for A Midsummer Night's Dream. I'd been to Sassari a month earlier to do workshop auditions to get a good cast in place and now is the moment of truth. The opening night is in four weeks' time at Sassari's largest theatre Teatro Verdi and I'm a bit nervous about directing a bunch of twenty-five assorted Sardinian artists. Some of them are professional actors and some of them are drama students of sorts but all of them speak Italian better than I do. We are scheduled to start at 5pm, after the obligatory siesta, at a place called Orfanotrofio Figlie Di Maria on Via Francesco Muroni in the east of the city. As in Britain the church has long been a good source of cheap rehearsal space as they own so much property many of which have halls, community centres or large function rooms attached.

Being English I'm unfashionably early and arrive well before kick-off at the large double gates of the address given to me on a scrap of paper the night before by the producer. I gingerly press the buzzer. For what seems like a lifetime I wait patiently resisting the temptation to ring again or light up a Camel. After another few minutes the addiction gets the better of me and I resign myself to having a smoke and waiting for the others to arrive at five. Of course no sooner have I taken the first puff than the gates swing open and I find myself staring at a disapproving nun who could not have been more than four feet high and a day under ninety. It was as if she had grown a centimetre a year since she was born. Without thinking, as if to test her disapproval threshold, I throw my cigarette on the floor and exhale 'buonasera'. Without a word she ushers me through the gates and into a fabulous courtyard filled with orange trees, lemon trees and plants of every variety – one of those real Mediterranean gardens that seem to only exist behind walls. I follow Yoda down a narrow pathway wondering if she is part of one of those orders that are forbidden to speak. This suits me fine. I'm not in the mood for religious chit chat and wouldn't know where to begin with any small talk in Italian let alone Latin.

We eventually pass through what appears to be some sort of annex with two huge stone baths in the middle of the room made of what looks like granite and lined with marble (I find out later they are 17th century). It does make you wonder if the nuns jump into the communal tubs for a bit of soap play after a game of footie in the courtyard. Finally the rehearsal room - which is actually a medium sized gymnasium. I thank my new friend who nods approvingly and shuffles out of the door. Crash mats, wooden bars and other gym related paraphernalia line the walls and I stand alone in the middle of the room staring at the basketball hoop further fuelling my imagination as to the sporting exploits of the order.

5pm comes and goes and I become suddenly aware of how nervous I really am. I'm no stranger to directing shows so why does this one make my stomach turn, hands tremble and my mouth feel like I'm sucking sandpaper? One of the most important jobs a director has is to coherently communicate a vision to his or her actors in order to achieve the end result. This seems relatively straight forward in English but in Italian? Will I be able to explain exactly what I mean? Is it really possible to do Shakespeare in a different language? Will everybody laugh at me? It's the fear of failure and the fear of the unknown. I am a stranger, an outsider, a culturally different animal with a different way of speaking who has traded the relative safety of his own country for a life in a foreign place that he doesn't know will work.

The door bangs open and in walks my producer, antiques dealer and friend Tommaso Sommo. 'Hello my brother', he bellows in English before giving me a big hug which does little to calm my nerves. *'Tutti sono in ritardo, tu sei in Italia adesso amico mio'.* This roughly translates as 'everyone's late and we'll probably be starting at 6'. I make a mental note to give everyone a lecture on the importance of punctuality naively thinking I can change the collective mind-set of an entire nation. Sure enough by 6pm we are ready to start. There are now some thirty people in the gymnasium and Tommaso calls for order. A deathly hush. I'm up. I consider bolting for the door but I can't move my legs, besides there are so many people I can't see where the door is. In reasonably bad Italian I start to outline my vision for *Sogno di una Notte di Mezza Estate*. Things are going well, people are nodding, nobody's laughing and my confidence is growing. I finish the introduction (admittedly with some help from a couple of cast members who speak good English) and end on a round of applause. Christ, I could do with a beer.

I call the actors for the first scene and get straight down to business. I've never been one for a sit down read through of the script preferring instead to get the play on its feet as quickly as possible. I have a copy of the text in English and in Italian so I can follow what the actors are saying even if I can't fully understand it. What strikes me immediately as odd is the translation in Italian. Where Shakespeare uses a rhyming couplet the translator follows suit but makes the ends of the lines rhyme regardless as to whether it makes any sense. I'm told that this is the case with most Shakespearian translations. It looks like I'm going to have to get the scissors out.

So I'm into the first scene and realise there is no actor playing Egeus – or Egeo in Italian. I call over Tommaso – *'Dov'è Egeo?'* *'Egeo?'* He replies. *'Sì, Egeo!'* I shout. Tommaso looks thoughtful and pulls out his mobile phone. After an extremely animated conversation ending in *Coglione* he turns to me and says *'L'attore non può più farlo, hai veramente bisogno di un Egeo?'* The actor can't do it any more do you really need an Egeus? *'Of course I need a fucking Egeus I can't do the play without a fucking Egeus!'* For those of you who are not familiar with the play Egeus is pretty fucking important! Tommaso understands my English perfectly. Whispers ripple around the gymnasium. This is not a good start. For the second time Tommaso pulls out his mobile phone and this time a less animated conversation ensues ending with *grazie mille.* Triumphantly he announces *'Ho trovato un Egeo, Carlo Valle'* – I've found an Egeus, Carlo Valle. At the mention of the name Carlo Valle excitement sweeps the room. Apparently Carlo is a local celebrity who has his own TV show called Aspirina. It's a Sardinian comedy show with two actors who do alternative voice overs for famous films. He'll be here in fifteen minutes. In Britain it is unheard of that an actor wouldn't show up for the first day of rehearsals without having first informed either the producer or director let alone be able to recast him within fifteen minutes. I've never met this Carlo and without giving him a proper audition it's a risk. I call a ten minute break and wait for Signor Valle. It turns out that Carlo is a very good actor, perfect for the part and a great person to boot. In fact all the actors are very good.

It's amazing that such a relatively small town can produce so much talent. Working with Italian actors as opposed to British ones is a refreshing experience. The Italians are naturally more physical and therefore more theatrical whereas the British tend to be more reserved physically putting the emphasis on the spoken word rather than the action. I breathe a sigh of relief and the rest of the session goes without a hitch. Despite the initial hiccup everyone is happy and there is a real atmosphere of excitement - of something good and different happening. I wonder how long my honeymoon period will last. This is no quick in and out, I am in this for the long haul and I need to continue working in Sardinia, this is my new home after all.

We finish at 10pm and head off to the local *spaghetteria* on Viale Italia for a well-deserved *cena* and of course the obligatory ice cold beer. I'm starving or as Tommaso so eloquently puts it 'I could eat a nun's arse through a convent gate'. My *Spaghetti al Nero di Seppia* is fantastic and my lecture on punctuality will have to wait until tomorrow.

Spaghetti al Nero di Seppia

Serves 4

Ingredients

- *600g fresh squid*
- *320g spaghetti*
- *80ml dry white wine*
- *1 tablespoon tomato paste diluted in a little water*
- *a small bunch parsley (minced)*
- *2 cloves of garlic (chopped)*
- *1/4 cup olive oil*
- *salt*
- *black pepper*

Preparation

Begin by cleaning the squid. Gently pull the head away from the tentacles, the entrails should come out at the same time. The ink sacks will be in the innards and are thin and silvery, about 2cms long. Be careful not to break them. Wash the squid well under cold water, chop the bodies and tentacles into small pieces. Open the ink sacks and deposit the ink in a bowl.

Heat the oil in a pan and sweat the garlic without letting it brown. Add the squid, the minced parsley, and a generous amount of freshly ground black pepper. Cover and simmer over low heat for approximately 45 minutes, checking every so often to make sure it's not sticking (add a little hot water if needed). Stir in the tomato sauce or paste with the white wine and add it to the pan. Simmer for a further 20 minutes, uncovered. Add a little hot water and simmer for another 15 minutes until the sauce is not too thick or too runny.

Bring 3 litres of water to the boil. Add salt and then the pasta. Stir the squid ink into the sauce. Drain the pasta when ready, stir into the sauce, and serve.

***

I'm woken up at 7.30am the following morning by what sounds like a brass band in the street below my window. A little worse for wear I stagger out of bed to investigate and sure enough there is a brass band playing beneath my window complete with uniforms, trumpets, trombones, tubers, drums and anything else a brass band should rightly have. It's seven-thirty in the morning for Christ's sake. I go back to bed only to be woken up fifteen minutes later by the peal of bells of every variety. There are four churches in close proximity to where I'm staying and all of them conspiratorially kick off at 7.45 in the morning - a reminder to get my arse out of bed and go and be a good Catholic. I resign myself to an early start and go out in search of that life blood of all Italians - coffee.

Today I need to concentrate on finding somewhere to live (the place I am in is fantastic and free but only available for the duration of the rehearsal period) so not starting work each day until 5pm suits my purpose just fine. Though the practice of such odd rehearsal hours is completely alien to me after the 9-5 rehearsal routine in London I am happy to use the time constructively and explore my new surroundings. There are scores of estate agents in Sassari and they work in much the same way as they do in the UK – they find you somewhere to live and take loads of money off you. I think it's a global thing. Not having much choice I do the rounds anyway to see what's on offer for the meagre budget I've set myself of 300 euros a month. Sassari is not a major tourist attraction like Alghero so I am hoping my paltry sum will suffice.

Estate agents in Italy usually take a month's rent for themselves, two months' rent deposit and a month's rent in advance - a total outlay of 1200 euros - up front. Good job theatre directors in Sassari get paid enormous amounts of money for their services. If I'm going to be here a while and serious about getting under the proverbial fingernails of a culture I want to live where the action is, I want to live in *centro storico.*

If you want to be an expatriate you have to take advantage of the historic centres that exist in almost every Italian town. Full of bars, restaurants, delis, shops, renaissance buildings, churches, haberdashers, cobblers, carpenters, museums and art galleries, they are by far the most interesting places to be. Or you could buy a house to restore in the country. My only other stipulation is to have a terrace. Because of the Mediterranean climate, terraces become another room, a space that you would use as much as say a living room or kitchen - a space to put your washing out, sunbath naked, barbeque, entertain, read, sleep, eat or even garden. Not surprisingly I'm told that they are at a premium in Sassari so I'm not overly optimistic. I start with the biggest agent in town on Via Rosello, Tecnocasa, whose name suggests I might end up living in an Acid House. I'm assured that it is a reputable national chain and completely legit so in I go. After filling in some forms and giving over my mobile phone number I'm told that they will be in touch as soon as they have something that meets my requirements. I repeat the process with a number of other agents and head off to explore the town.

What you immediately notice about Sassari is that it's all up hill (of course that does depend, obviously, from which direction you are coming from but if you are arriving by bus, train or from the airport then you will arrive at the bottom of the hill at the start of Corso Vittorio Emanuele – the town's main drag). I start at the bottom and slowly make my way up. It's hot and hard work made more difficult by the fact that they are digging up Il Corso to upgrade the sewage system and lay mains gas pipes. All the houses and apartments are reliant on bottled gas and the sewage system is an old network of small vaulted tunnels - pretty to look at but no longer functional. Apparently there is European money to re-do the entire underground infrastructure by 2012.

Pile upon pile upon pile of huge medieval flagstones line the street all numbered in blue or red supposedly to put them back in the order in which they were taken out. One massive jigsaw. I hope the numbers aren't written in chalk as rain is forecast for later. The main street is full of shops of all shapes and sizes as well as some beautiful medieval doorways and gothic windows. Narrow alleyways take you off into the crumbling, jumbled maze of backstreets and small piazzas that riddle the old town centre. Senegalese, Chinese and Italians live side by side packed tightly into the *piccoli vicoli* that make up the warren that is *il centro storico*. Aromas abound bombarding the casual tourist with familiar and unfamiliar smells; fried fish, roasting meat, boiling stock - almost every doorway and every window letting slip the culture that exists within. The sound of French, African, Sassarese, Sardinian, Italian and Chinese completes this rich multi-ethnic, multilingual tapestry that makes up the lower part of the historic centre.

Not surprisingly I'm hungry and head off to the nearest café for a *tramezzino* and cold beer. For those of you who have never encountered the *tramezzino* it's a triangular, crust less, Italian sandwich on soft white bread filled with any number of delicious things. Popular filling combinations include: *tonno e insalata, tonno e pomodoro, prosciutto e formaggio, pomodoro e mozzarella, prosciutto e funghi, gamberi e insalata, uovo e pomodoro* or *uovo e insalata.* Normally a couple of them suffice and washed down with a cold Ichnusa beer make the perfect light lunch. Ichnusa is the beer of choice in Sardinia. Brewed on the island since 1912 in the southern town of Assemini near Cagliari it is a crisp blond beer (4.7 % ABV) and a wonderful thirst quencher on a hot day. It gets its name from the ancient Greek name for Sardinia - Hyknusa. The dark brown bottle proudly bears the unmistakable Sardinian flag called *I Quattro Mori* (The Four Moors' flag consists of a red cross on a white background with a Moor's head in each corner). Ichnusa is now owned by Heineken but thankfully that doesn't affect the taste. I forego the *tramezzino* when I see the lunch offering - *Gnocchetti Sardi.* When in Rome...

Gnocchetti Sardi

Gnocchetti (also known as malloreddus) are a small, concave pasta with a ribbed back made with pure durum wheat semolina.

Serves 4

Ingredients

- *400g Sardinian gnocchetti*
- *salt and pepper to taste*
- *6 tablespoons olive oil*
- *1 small onion, finely chopped*
- *1 clove of garlic (chopped)*
- *300g fresh Italian sausage, meat removed from the skin and crumbled*
- *35g dried porcini, soaked for half an hour, then finely chopped (keep the liquid)*
- *3 tablespoons dry white wine*
- *600g polpa di pomodoro (crushed tomatoes)*

Preparation

Heat the oil in a non-stick pan, add the onion and let cook until soft. Add the garlic and cook for another minute and then add the sausage and porcini. Stir until the meat is brown then add the wine and tomato pulp. Cook over a very low heat for about 45 minutes. If it starts to look too dry add a little of the mushroom water. When ready season to taste with salt and pepper. Cook the pasta in plenty of boiling salted water until al dente, about 10 - 12 minutes.

Mix the pasta with the sauce, sprinkle with grated pecorino and serve immediately.

***

Hoping the band stops for lunch and the church bells don't chime the 24 hour clock I head back to base for a little *pisolino* before rehearsals at 5pm.

I say rehearsals at 5pm but as usual we don't get under way until six. I give everyone a stern lecture on punctuality and responsibility pointing out that they wouldn't be late on stage so why be late for rehearsals. That'll teach them.

The evening goes well and we finish as usual at 10pm. Tonight we're heading for another Pizzeria, El Burladero, this time in a shopping centre on the edge of town. Hmm, sounds lovely. Tommaso explains that the Pizzeria is one of the sponsors of the show and we're obliged to eat there at least three or four times a week. I'm going to turn into a *Quattro Stagioni*. Once you've passed through the *centro commerciale* the place isn't that bad, in fact once you are inside you could be in any pizzeria anywhere in Italy. As usual almost everyone is there and the atmosphere is great. Twenty-five Sardinians really know how to enjoy themselves.

Tonight I'm feeling daring and going for the *Diavola* - a combination of tomato, mozzarella, green peppers, peperoni, onions and the obligatory *olio piccante*. Fantastic.

Olio Piccante

Sardinians like most Italians don't like their food spicy but are partial to a hot spicy oil now and again. Every pizzeria will have a bottle on hand to drizzle over pizza as will most restaurants.

I bought fresh chillies and hung them to dry for a month but you can always just use chilli flakes.

Ingredients

- *1 litre of olive oil (doesn't have to be extra virgin)*
- *40g of chilli flakes*

Preparation

If you are using fresh dried chillies they need to be finely chopped into flakes. You can use a blender to speed things up. Gently heat the oil in a large pan but not until boiling point. When the oil is nice and hot add the chilli flakes and simmer for 3-4 minutes. Add 2 or three whole chillies for good measure. Let the oil cool for 10 minutes before decanting into bottles ensuring all the flakes go in. Seal the bottles and let rest for 3-4 days before using. We used a sterilized wine bottle for the mixture but any sterilized glass receptacle will do as long as you can put a top on it.

The more flakes you add the hotter the oil.

It's funny that even here in a shopping centre the pizza is wood fired, it makes such a difference to the overall taste and most Italians wouldn't accept anything less, least of all the electric oven rubbish that we get back home. It really is good but I hope eating pizza four nights a week doesn't put me off for life. Especially life in Italy where pizza is a national dish and extremely hard to avoid.

Tommaso picks up the tab and we head back into town for a nightcap or *La Staffa* as the Italians call it. *La Staffa* is Italian for stirrup so this is quite literally the 'one for the road'. That last drink when you're sitting in the saddle before riding your horse pissed back home.

There is no better way of seeing a place than hanging out with the locals and the Sards are a great bunch of people to hang out with. Since I arrived I have been welcomed as one of them not feeling for a moment like an outsider, testament to their wonderful hospitality and sense of openness. I could get used to this. Rather than risk being pulled over drunk in charge of a *cavallo* I leave my horse at the bar and decide to walk the short distance home. Sassari looks beautiful at night - the medieval streets and piazzas bathed in the orange hue of the somewhat Victorian style street lamps. It's 2 o'clock in the morning on a warm September night and the town is fast asleep. The only sound - my footsteps on the cobbled stones. I get into bed and dream of pizza.

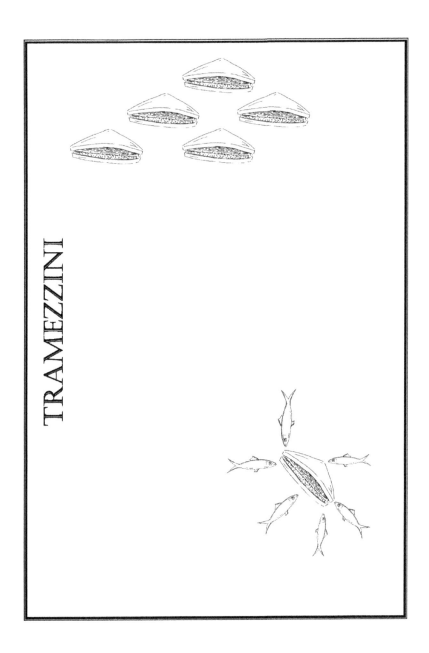

TRAMEZZINI

CHAPTER THREE

What now? It's my mobile ringing (a poor substitute for the conspiracy of bells). 9.30am, I can't believe I slept through the *campanili* – quite an achievement. I answer the phone, '*Pronto?*' It's Tecnocasa. They have an apartment for me to see at 11am on the corner of Viale Umberto and Via Fancello. I arrive ten minutes early and have a quick recce of the area. It's not exactly in the centre but more on the fringes of the old town with not much to offer in the way of bars restaurants or shops. The buildings are old and beautiful so I decide to reserve judgment until I've been inside. The agent arrives bang on eleven wearing the obligatory suit and tie. He would have looked right at home in London if he hadn't arrived on a moped. The pleasantries are brief and he leads me down a small side street and to my disappointment a relatively new looking apartment block. We take the lift to the third floor and enter a very small studio flat no bigger than fifty square meters. In Italy all property is measured in square meters unlike the UK where everything is in feet so this would roughly be about 530 square feet.

I have a feeling this isn't what I'm looking for and confirmation comes as he gives me the grand tour. When I say grand tour I mean walking around in a circle in what is essentially a bed-sit. The main living area consists of a bed, table, chairs, *angolo cucina* (which literally translates as corner kitchen) and a double glazed window – the sort that you can only open half way. The worst part is the ceiling covered in large tacky polystyrene tiles. I couldn't imagine lying in bed at night looking up at those. A mirror might be tacky but at least it serves a purpose.

We part company and I promise to think about it albeit for a mille-second. The rent is 250 euros so well within my budget just not within my grand design. I need to live right in the historic heart of the city, I want somewhere with character and I have to have that highly sought after outside space. I want to live the Mediterranean dream not dream the dream and a compromise so early on would not bode well for the future. At least the price gives me a glimmer of hope that there is something out there just waiting for me and my telly.

Rehearsals go well for the rest of the week apart from the punctuality thing. They are getting better and we seem to be starting at 5.30pm which I suppose is some sort of progress. I'm determined to get us starting on time by the end of the process if it kills me, which it probably will. A welcome break from pizza comes at the weekend in the form of

Agriturismo. Agritourism has seen a major growth in the past few years as a unique, affordable way to eat and sleep your way around Italy. Compared to a farm holiday in Britain this is something very different. Most, if not all, Agritourism places offer accommodation but I've found that it's often the food and the locations that make these places special. Usually found in the middle of the Italian countryside these are working farms producing most of the ingredients that you will find on your plate in the evening. They are places to relax and enjoy the surroundings without having to get up at five in the morning to milk cows or collect eggs. Some Agritourism farms are more chic than others often with swimming pools and nicer rooms and this is reflected in the price.

Most offer outdoor pursuits such as horseback riding or guided walks none of which are obligatory if you just want to sit back, relax and be treated like royalty. Some farms will even offer cookery classes or wine tasting if that's your tipple. According to the news agency Reuters nearly 16,000 small farms opened their doors to holidaymakers last year with another 700 expected to join them this year. Farming incomes across Europe have shown a steep decline over the past decade and more and more people are turning to Agritourism to subsidise their income. Italy alone saw an income fall in agricultural revenue by 4% in 2006 and that increases every year.

Sa Mandra is located within spitting distance of Alghero airport (not the most likely setting for an Agritourism farm), five kilometres from Alghero itself and twenty-five kilometres from Sassari.

My host for the evening is drama student and antique shop owner Licia Provvisionato (her real name is Felicia meaning happy in Italian but she prefers the shorter version and I can't say I blame her). Licia's English is fluent which is just as well as relying on my Italian for interesting conversation would make for a very dull evening. The table is booked for 8pm and we arrive early to have a look around. Despite its close proximity to the airport it's very beautiful. The tables are set and waiting in a sprawling garden bursting with flowers, plants and trees for shade. Unfortunately for the green fingered reader I'm horticulturally challenged otherwise I would love to list all the different varieties. In one corner sits a *Pinnetta*, a traditional Sardinian round house with a thatched peaked roof that I'm told you can eat in during the winter. In the opposite corner one of the biggest open fire barbeques I have ever seen plays host to five sizzling suckling pigs. The smell is absolutely wonderful and my stomach groans with delight as I wipe the drool from my chin. The king of Sardinian dishes, Suckling Pig (*Porcheddu* in Sardinian) is a traditional favourite eaten in large quantities all over the island.

PORCETTO ARROSTO

Porcetto Arrosto

Preparation

There are two methods for cooking Porcetto Arrosto – the traditional way over an open fire (obviously you need the outside space) or in the oven. You can order a pig from any good butcher and it will need to be between 15 and 20kg for outside roasting and approximately 10kg for oven cooking. The preparation is the same for both. Remove all the interior parts of the pig (liver, lungs, heart etc.) and then clean thoroughly with water. Dry the meat well with kitchen towel. Rub salt all over the skin and inside the cavity making sure the pig is well covered.

The traditional way - The pig should be put on a very large skewer and roasted approximately half a meter away from the flames and continually rotated. Unlike traditional barbecues it is important for the flavour that the meat is cooked on flames as opposed to coal. You will need a lot of wood. In Sardinia they use a slow burning wood such as olive. If you have a motorised spit turning device it will make life easier as patience and skill are required when turning the meat to make sure it doesn't burn. The pig is ready when you stick a skewer into the thickest part of the meat and no juices run out. There are no precise timings as it depends on the size of

*pig, type of wood etc. but you need to allow a good few hours.
A quicker way to cook the pig is to cut it in half lengthways so
you are left with half the head and half the hind quarters on
one side and the same on the other.*

*Not everyone has access to an open fire but great results can
be achieved using your normal kitchen oven. Obviously make
sure the pig will fit before buying it and make sure it won't
touch the sides of the oven. Pre-heat the oven to 160 degrees
and cook the pig for approximately three hours or until
beautifully golden. Basting the meat with lard every so often
will bring out the colour.*

***

I'm famished, ravenous, starving, dog hungry and can't wait
to get stuck in. We are shown to our table and wait patiently
for the festivities to begin. There is no menu and it's a fixed
price, you eat whatever they give you which I'm told is a lot
with plenty of choice. Good. Wine and water arrive
automatically followed close behind by the *Antipasti*:
Salsiccia e formaggio (salami and cheese), *Coppa e pancetta*
(salt cured pork and rolled, seasoned pancetta), *Prosciutto
Monte Spada* (ham from Mount Spada), *Crema di formaggio
al timo* (cream cheese with thyme*), sott'oli della casa*

(preserved vegetables in extra virgin olive oil) and *Coratella alla Barbaricina* (from the region of Barbagia and not for the squeamish, *Coratella* is the Italian word for the organs inside the chest cavity of small animals like lambs, chickens and rabbits). The stuff just keeps on coming, plate after plate, surely enough to feed a family of six for a week let alone two people. It's all delicious and of course the little devil in one ear is saying 'go on eat it all' but thankfully the little angel in the other tells me there's a lot more to come and advises restraint.

Everything comes with *Carasau,* a wafer thin, circular, crisp, Sardinian bread also known as *carta da musica* (music paper) because of its form – not its taste. It was created in the region of Barbagia by shepherds who needed a bread that would last longer when they were off for days tending their flocks. *Carasatura* means literally 'a double cooking'. Apparently *Carasau* is a major contributor to the high life expectancy of Sardinians. According to the BBC - 'something remarkable links the remote Japanese island of Okinawa and the small Sardinian mountain town of Ovodda. Okinawa has a population of one million and of those 900 are centenarians, four times higher than the average in Britain or America. Even more remarkably, Ovodda is the only region in the world where as many men as women live to be 100 years of age.' This small town has a resident population of just over

1,700 and boasts five centenarians. I order more *Carasau* and contemplate moving to Ovodda.

Not surprisingly with our mouths continually full of food conversation is slow but Licia does tell me a few interesting facts about antiques in Sardinia. She buys all her antiques in Newark near Nottingham! Every two months Licia and five other dealers from the island get on a Ryanair flight from Alghero to Stansted and buy British antiques at the bi-monthly antiques fair in Newark-on-Trent. They share the cost of an articulated lorry (hired from a company in Sardinia) and ship the antiques back to the island via France then Genoa. Would you believe it? I suppose if you're a Sardinian antiques dealer you probably would. 'So, what sort of stuff do you buy?' I ask. 'Oh, you know the usual – Sheffield plate, silver, Victorian furniture, Edwardian furniture, porcelain, jewellery, paintings and when I can get it Georgian' she replies. If my mouth wasn't already full of Antipasti it would have been gobsmacked. If the average articulated lorry has a capacity of 50 cubic meters that's 300 cubic meters of British antiques being sold on the island every year.

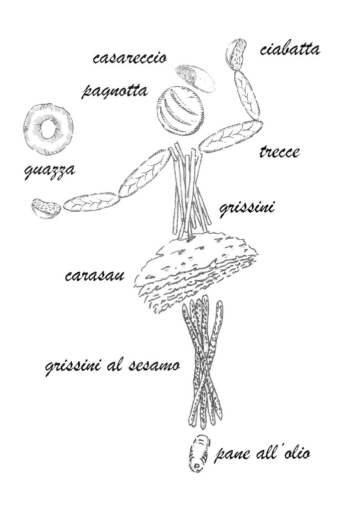

casareccio

ciabatta

pagnotta

guazza

trecce

grissini

carasau

grissini al sesamo

pane all'olio

PANE

The next course arrives, the *Primi Piatti*: *Ravioli alle sette erbe con pomodorini freschi e basilico* (seven herb ravioli with fresh baby tomatoes and basil) and *Maharrones de Pungiu al sugo di vitello* (pasta from Pungiu with veal sauce). I've died and gone to heaven, the food is just wonderful and the only problem is whether I can finish it or not. I eat on as Licia continues to feed me interesting facts about the island and as the wine disappears my Italian seems to improve. And yes, contrary to popular British belief people from Sardinia are not called sardines but Sards.

The Italian antiques market here is apparently quite small. People don't want to hang on to the old stuff that reminds them of the past; particularly the post-war, post Mussolini years. Most people have replaced old furniture with new which is why Italian antiques are harder to find and why the market consists mainly of English and French. Not three kilometres from where we sit is the 'new town' of Fertilia built by Mussolini in the 1930's as a port to rival that of Venice. Needless to say his plan didn't work out but the large church in the town centre is still called San Marco and the square is called Piazza Venezia Giulia.

I'm stuffed, full, bursting, bloated, and don't think I can eat anymore. Then the *Secondi Piatti* arrive: *Brasato di agnellone al finocchietto selvatico* (slow cooked braised lamb with wild fennel) *Porcetto Arrosto* (spit roast suckling pig)

Verdure di stagione (seasonal vegetables). Against my better judgement I try it all and as I suspected - marvellous. The lamb is simple and exceptional and here, according to the chef, is how you do it:

Brasato di agnellone al finocchietto selvatico

Serves 4

Ingredients:
- *1kg of lamb*
- *200g of fresh tomatoes*
- *1 clove of garlic*
- *1 medium onion*
- *salt*
- *wild fennel*

Preparation:
Wash and boil the fennel until soft. Retain the cooking water. Cut the lamb into small pieces and fry in oil with garlic and onion. When the meat is half cooked add the fennel and tomatoes and continue cooking on a low heat. Pour in the fennel water a little at a time until the meat is cooked through.

FINOCCHIO SELVATICO

We both give in and decide to call it a night. We gave it our best shot and we're pretty proud of our achievements, making it to the end of the meat course was no mean feat. We finish the last of the wine and ask for the bill. To our complete astonishment the waitress refuses to bring it over making it very clear that we will offend the establishment if we don't complete the courses. What?! I look at Licia and then the waitress who has that expression which says 'you ain't going anywhere soon mate'. What do we do? We have no choice. Licia politely asks how much is left to come. '*Ricotta con Miele* (ricotta with honey), *frutta* (fruit), *Dolci Sardi* (Sardinian cakes), *Sevada* (Large sweet ravioli), *digestivo e caffè* (digestive and coffee)' the waitress replies. Oh, not much then. Resigned, we wait for the remaining courses and just hope we can make a good enough job of them and not offend the management.

We struggle through and finally make it to the end and as if winning some kind of trophy we are then presented with the bill. I feel like jumping up and making a speech but am conscious that any sudden movement might mean the dinner revisited. We pay the very reasonable sum of sixty euros between two of us and very, very slowly make our way to the car.

The short drive to Sassari takes twenty five minutes and I can't wait to get to bed and start sleeping off some of the seventeen dishes I've consumed throughout the evening. I thank Licia for her great company and head for the pillow. I certainly don't dream of food.

It's Sunday and I wake up late knowing that all I have to do today is work on digesting the night before. It's another very hot day and I contemplate finding my way to the nearest beach but opt instead to stay in Sassari and have a very lazy *giorno*. What I didn't bargain for was the complete emptiness of the historic centre on a Sunday. There is virtually nothing open apart from churches and I do feel sorry for the odd tourist wandering around trying to find a bite to eat or a cold drink. Map and good book in hand I head off for the tranquillity of the public gardens for a read and possible *pisolino* in the shade. Between Corso Margherita di Savoia and Viale Pasquale Stanislao Mancini the gardens are beautiful and complete with therapeutic sounding fountains ideal for the world weary traveller and a bit of R&R. Seduced by the soft welcoming grass I nod off within seconds. It's been a long week and the steep learning curve is taking its toll.

I wake up with a start and realise I've been asleep for almost two hours! I quickly check for dribble and make sure nobody has stolen my trousers or tied my shoe laces together before heading back into town for a *tramezzino* and

Sardinia's answer to the Pork Pie – *Panadas*. I can't believe I'm hungry.

Panadas

Panadas, or Impanadas, are small meat pies and one of Sardinia's signature dishes. And they do look like pork pies. This particular recipe is from the region of Cuglieri.

Serves 6 - 8

Ingredients - The filling

- *350g stewing beef*
- *350g lean pork*
- *250g artichoke hearts*
- *100g fresh fava beans*
- *100g pitted black olives, chopped*
- *100 ml olive oil*
- *glass of Sardinian Vernaccia, or other strong dry white wine*
- *2 cloves of garlic, peeled and chopped*
- *small bunch parsley, chopped*
- *pinch of freshly ground nutmeg*
- *pinch of saffron*
- *2-3 sun dried tomatoes - if packed in oil, drain well*

The Dough

- *1kg flour*
- *200g rendered lard*
- *olive oil*
- *20g salt*
- *1 beaten egg*

Preparation

Finely dice the beef and pork. Sauté the meat, stirring in the olive oil and when browned add the Vernaccia, the spices, herbs, artichokes and fava beans. Cook, stirring, until the Vernaccia has evaporated but the mixture remains moist. Add the olives and let the filling rest for two hours.

Mix the flour, lard, salt and enough warm water to make a dough. Knead well and when ready roll into a sheet about 5mm thick. From the dough make fifteen 8cm and fifteen 4cm diameter circles (or as many as you can).

Put a large spoonful of filling in the centre of each of the larger circles, fold the edges up around the filling, and seal the balls with the smaller discs. Crimp the dough to make sure the pieces stick together. Preheat the oven to 180 degrees. Put the Panadas on greaseproof paper and bake for 45 minutes. Remove from the oven and brush with beaten egg. Serve hot or cold.

CHAPTER FOUR

The cast and I seem to have come to some sort of unspoken compromise over rehearsals. As if tipping their collective hat to me wanting to start at 5pm but not wanting to completely give up their national identity we start at 5.15pm for the rest of the week. I've gained forty five minutes of ground but still want that illusive fifteen minutes. The good working vibe continues for the next five days as does the pizza, Ichnusa and *La Staffa.* My post-apocalyptic vision for the play is going down well. It's Rocky Horror meets Mad Max meets classical Shakespeare. A bold departure for Sassari, a town accustomed to more traditional interpretations of classic plays. I'll either be shot or crowned but I hold firm, committed to my direction.

I see two other apartments during the week (courtesy of Tecnocasa) but neither of them are what I'm looking for - the first being too modern and the second being too expensive. Both Licia and Tommaso have offered me a place to stay so I'm not overly worried about not finding a flat in time.

It's the weekend again and we're off to the beach to catch the last of the good September weather. There's a group of us going and complete with picnic we pile into various vehicles to make the short trip to Sassari's nearest *spiaggia* - Platamona.

Platamona, also known as the Sassari Riviera, is north of the city, east of Porto Torres and takes about twenty minutes by car. Being so close to Sassari it's packed at the weekend with city dwellers escaping the heat and grime of the town for the relative sanctuary of the sea. The beach is huge. From Porto Torres to Valledoria it stretches almost nineteen kilometres as far as the eye can see. Of course the stretch nearest to Sassari is heaving but I'm told if you go a kilometre further up you practically have the entire beach to yourself.

We make towel camp at a place called La Rotonda close to the various bars and restaurants that cater for the thousands of tanned sun worshippers. The majority of the buildings are in need of serious repair having been built in the 50's and 60's and not maintained since. This particular stretch of sand comes under the jurisdiction of two councils (Sassari and Sorso) that can't agree on how to develop the area so the buildings will probably stay like this until they finally fall down. It's not the best bit of beach in the world but hey, who cares, it's a beach.

I suddenly become very conscious of my lack of colour. The Sards have had all summer to work up a good tan and I have a lot of catching up to do but I know it'll take me a day to go red and then a month to go brown. The good thing is they know you are English so it's taken for granted that you're going to be pale but this does little to diminish my self-consciousness. And how is it that the Italians appear perfectly dressed on the beach already in swimming attire (that you never see them put on) and I have to hop around on one leg with my towel falling off? Is it something they learn at school like the green cross code? And they are all so beautiful – bronzed, no cellulite and with very fit bodies. So that's why they're always late for rehearsals, they've been down the gym. I make a mental note to myself if I'm still here next year: (1) go to the gym (2) do some secret pre-tanning (3) get my back waxed.

I put on the 'Factor 20' and head for the water. It's wonderfully clear and warm and I have to pinch myself. Have I really moved to Sardinia? Do I really live on this island paradise in the middle of the Mediterranean? It still seems unreal but at the same time the most natural thing in the world. I remind myself there's a lot to do if I'm serious about making a life here.

To the north you can just make out the French island of Corsica and to the west the small Sardinian island of Asinara.

This tiny land mass is the only known habitat of a miniature, white, albino donkey from which the island gets its name. Asinara used to be a penal colony in the 1800's and a prison camp during the Second World War for Austrian and Hungarian soldiers and remained a prison until 1998 housing mafia members and terrorists. The most famous being Salvatore Totò Riina (also known as the short one) who, being the head of the Corleonese crime family in Sicily, was charged with the murder of anti-mafia judge Falcone in 1992.

Asinara is now a heavily protected national park where swimming is permitted on only three beaches, docking a boat is forbidden and construction is definitely a big no. So, if you want to build a house on the beach with private jetty and barbeque miniature ass, think again. The island now has some seven hundred inhabitants - plus the donkeys of course whose numbers are slowly diminishing, hopefully not in a sizzling blaze of glory.

I swim the four meters back to shore for a spot of well-deserved lunch (I had, after all, been exercising). *Panini, prosciutto, mortadella, pomodori* and *pecorino* make for an excellent beach picnic (is it only the English that manage to get sand in their food? Maybe they learn that at school here as well - the sandless sandwich). Despite the 'Factor 20' my skin is feeling a little tender and I try to stay in the shade as much as possible but my enthusiasm for the beach life gets the better of me and I start to turn a little red. Another mental note for next year: (4) buy total sun block and re-think mental note (2). The rest of the afternoon goes as one might expect, sunbathing, swimming, chatting and a bit of bat and ball, all playing their part in what is turning out to be a thoroughly enjoyable day. With nothing to do in Sassari on a Sunday this is definitely how I'll spend my weekends next year – if I'm still here.

The next day brings good news. One of the cast members has called saying that a friend of his has a flat in *centro storico*. It will become available in a month and because there is no agent involved the upfront money will be less. And it has a terrace. I have an appointment that morning and despite the sun burn excitedly get myself ready. I've called Licia and she's promised to go with me just in case there are any problems with the language.

We meet at the given address, Via Largo Infermeria San Pietro and scan the area. It's right in the centre on the top floor of an old building and close to everything. Perfect. We climb the four stories via an old slate staircase and arrive huffing and puffing at a small, green, arched wooden door and press the buzzer marked Ilaria. I have a good feeling about this. A bohemian looking woman in her mid-thirties answers the door and after brief introductions we're invited in. A small hallway with a spacious bathroom to the left gives way to a beautiful open plan space complete with fireplace and pitched roof. This in turn gives way to a small kitchen but plenty big enough for one person. A wooden spiral staircase goes up to a wooden mezzanine floor which is the bedroom and from the bedroom another small arched doorway takes you out onto the terrace. The views are fantastic. In one direction you can see all the way to Porto Torres and the Gulf of Asinara and in the other a spectacular vista of the historic centre including the unique façade of Il Duomo. The flat is minimally furnished with simple units, table, chairs, small sofa and ample storage space. The furniture is nothing special but perfectly adequate for what I need. The walls are all white with plenty of woodwork to give it a warmer feel in the winter. In fact if I were to design a small bachelor pad it would probably look something like this one. It's just what I've been looking for with the added bonus of a wood burning fire place. Licia tells me the apartment is called a *mansarda* which means loft in Italian and even Licia admits she has never seen one quite as nice as this one. Now the big question – how much does it cost? '350 euro a month' Ilaria says. Yes! Yes! Yes! OK, it's fifty euros more than my budget but what the hell, this is too good an opportunity to pass up and I'll never find another flat like it for less. Ilaria tells me she's just bought a house and should be able to move in about a month and in the meantime I should contact the landlord to sort out the contract. The owner's name is Marco Sanna and she gives me the number.

In Sassari people like to pass on good flats to people they know, people who come recommended which probably explains my lack of success with the agents. I feel very privileged to be recommended and thank Ilaria for her kindness before heading down the stairs and into Largo Infermeria San Pietro, my soon to be new address. Licia promises to phone Marco to set up an appointment for later that week and, if available, tag along as well. I thank her profusely for her kindness. What you realise immediately when moving to another country is how completely and utterly reliant you are on other people. It's a feeling of helplessness. Your independence is compromised, your self-confidence is half what it was and the reality of being in a culture you don't know with a language you barely speak makes you feel small, almost naive. The profuse thanking of people is the acknowledgment that quite literally you can't survive without them.

I have a design meeting today and even this familiar theatrical territory feels slightly alien to me. This isn't England, things are done the Sardinian way and you have to understand and accept the differences even if you don't necessarily agree with them.

We are ten days away from technical rehearsals and I need to make sure that Tommaso is on top of the stage design. Unlike in Britain where the designer comes up with a design based on the director's vision, here the designer or *scenografo* is the person who actually builds the design created by the director. On numerous occasions I had asked Tommaso for the design budget for set, costumes and props and the numerous replies have always been the same - 'don't worry my friend just tell me what you want, if we can't afford it I will let you know'. Maybe there is no money? I go through the list of things I'd asked for. I need three wrecked cars at the back of the stage (one stage right, one stage left and the third to create a bridge between the other two). Tommaso tells me we have one car and he's looking for the other two. I ask him about the music. My idea is to have a DJ mix the music live on stage rather than have someone operate the sound from a box. 'We have Davide Merlini, the most famous DJ in all of Sassari' he replies. I ask him whether he's had any luck finding someone that can break-dance. 'We have Roberto Chessa the most famous break-dancer in all of Sardinia' (Apparently Roberto was Italy's national break-dancing champion). Finally the guitarist. I needed somebody to come on stage and serenade Hermia on behalf of Lysander. 'We have Jack Evans, the most famous guitarist on all the island'. Jack Evans? Sounds English to me. Indeed Jack is an Englishman from Tipton in the Black Country who moved here fifteen years ago when he met an Italian girl and they had a baby. Small world. Well everything seems to be under control and I can't wait to meet some of these people.

As if by magic and with perfect timing the door swings open revealing a tall back-lit silhouetted man with a guitar case. I kid you not, the moment only needed a bit of smoke and it would have been the perfect entrance. Jack Evans I presume? Either that or I'm just about to be gunned down in cold blood by Italy's secret theatre police – the STP. The STP or *Polizia Teatrale* would make six different types of police in Italy including *Vigili Urbani* (municipal police), *La Polizia* (general police), *Carabinieri* (military police), the *Gaurdia di Finanza* (finance police) and the *Guardia Forestale* (environmental police).

'Ello me ol' mucker' says Jack by way of introduction in a heavy Black Country accent. Jack is fifty two years old, has grey hair with grey goatee beard, wears round tinted glasses, pointy black shoes, black jeans, black waistcoat, white granddad collar shirt, long black leather jacket and wouldn't look at all out of place at a Memphis blues convention or in a Johnny Cash tribute band. He is so not Italian and his *Buongiorno* to Tommaso with heavy Tipton lilt confirms the fact. Despite the accent Jack's Italian is very good which I suppose it would be after fifteen years. We get down to business and I explain to him exactly what I need. It turns out that Jack really is a good guitarist as he reels off his biog from what he calls 'the old days back home'. He used to play with the Steve Gibbons band, Robert Plant and even supported The Who in Germany on a couple of occasions. What's he doing here then? (I could ask myself the same question). 'Ah you know, I was touring Europe and ended up in Sardinia, fell in love with a girl called Arianna and we now have a beautiful daughter called Effi. You can't beat Sardinia for the climate, good food and wine. What's there to go back to in England? – bloody rain that's what!' I have to admire Jack, he is a truly free spirit going exactly where his heart takes him for better or for worse. 'If I go to hell I'll go playing the guitar' he says in the immortal words of Jerry Lee Lewis (except he played the piano not the guitar).

It's good to talk to another Englishman, they do say, after all, that there is safety in numbers. Rehearsals start and I make a mental note to call Tommaso in the morning to remind him of the things that need to be done ASAP. The clock is ticking and in Sardinia it always seems to tick a little slower. I avoid the obligatory Pizza at the end of the session and head towards a restaurant called Il Castello in Piazza Azuni looking for fish. I'm not disappointed.

Gamberi alla Vernaccia

Serves 4

Ingredients

- *1kg king prawns in their shells*
- *1/2 cup of olive oil*
- *1 clove of garlic*
- *salt*
- *1/2 teaspoon chilli pepper*
- *250ml of Vernaccia (or similar dry, crisp white wine such as Vermentino)*

Preparation

Rinse the prawns thoroughly under running water. Remove the antennae and legs that could come off while cooking and rinse again.

Finely chop the garlic and parsley and mix with the chilli pepper and olive oil in a cup.

Place the prawns in a baking tray to form one layer without empty spaces. Sprinkle salt generously over the prawns and then evenly pour over the mixture.

Put the tray in a pre-heated oven at 170°C and let the prawns cook for 5 minutes.

After 5 minutes add the Vernaccia evenly and cover with foil. Let the prawns cook in the oven for another 8-10 minutes.

I'm sitting opposite Joe Pesci and he's asking me if I think he's funny? 'Do you think I'm funny? Do you think I'm fucking funny, you think I'm fucking funny don't you?' I'm nervous, it looks like Joe could explode into a violent rage any second now. 'Do you think I'm fucking funny, am I here to amuse you?' he repeats with more vigour. I'm trembling and I think I'm about to cry when I hear a familiar comforting voice – 'leave him be he's one of us, he's a good fellow'. It's Jack Evans, Jack Evans has come to rescue me. I wake up sweating, which isn't difficult in Sardinia, and breathe heavily.

I'm not one for Freudian dream interpretation but I do wonder who or what Jack is saving me from. Is it myself? Is it this island? Or is it Joe 'Fishy' Pesci and my insatiable appetite for Martin Scorsese films? I lie awake for a while wondering if *the interpretation of dreams is the royal road to knowledge of the unconscious activities of the mind* but I'm soon fast asleep again.

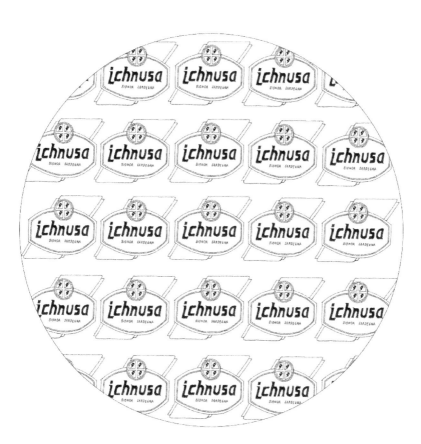

BIONDA SARDEGNA

CHAPTER FIVE

I wake up early determined to put Tommaso under some pressure to get things moving on the production front. I pick up my *telefonino* and dial his number...no answer. I have the address of his shop on a piece of paper and decide to pay him a surprise visit hoping he's not too busy to discuss the urgent business of show making. The address is on Via Turritana not far from where I'm staying and will take less than five minutes to get there on foot. It's a beautiful morning and the town basks resplendent in the late summer sun as I make my way through the labyrinth of tiny streets and up past Il Duomo di San Nicola.

Il Duomo is a truly spectacular piece of architecture dominating the sky line of *il centro storico* with its extravagant seventeenth-century Baroque façade. To call the frontage of this ecclesiastical shrine flamboyant would be an understatement (I tried to count all the stone carved heads once but lost count after sixty). In contrast the basic church itself is a much simpler Aragonese-Gothic structure of the fifteenth and sixteenth centuries. Its interior reflects the exterior, both having been spared the full Baroque treatment. The even older thirteenth century *Campanile* sits alongside the main construction sporting an array of gargoyles and gothic features. Definitely worth a look if you're in this part of the world.

Via Turritana is a long, narrow cobbled street stretching all the way from Il Duomo in the south of the historic centre to Via Brigata Sassari in the north. It used to be the gold and silver centre of the city and still has a number of jewellers and watchmakers keeping up the tradition. A perfect location for an antiques shop.

As I approach number forty-three I go through my mental check list making sure I have everything covered. It's not so much a confrontation that I want to have with Tommaso but more of a confirmation. I don't want to play the big director coming in from the outside (especially from another country) shouting and telling people what to do but, from experience, I know that certain things can't be left to the last minute and I get the impression that in Sardinia that is exactly what happens – at least in show business. Everybody has been so welcoming and I want to repay them by giving them the best show I possibly can even if it does mean pushing everyone a little harder and lightly kicking some *sederi*. Ah, number forty-three. It's shut. It's 10.30am on a Tuesday morning how can he be shut? A conspicuously small hand written note attached to the inside of the door with Blu-

Tack says *torno subito* that I take to mean 'back soon', but how soon? I try his *telefonino*...no answer.

On the corner about a hundred yards up the street I notice a small bar and decide to wait it out there while enjoying a *Cappuccino* and a read of the local rag. The bar is called *Gustaviños* (the wine taster) and as well as coffee and assorted daily journals has a healthy selection of Sardinian plonk. I pick out La Nuova Sardegna, the local newspaper of choice in the north of the island (L'Unione Sarda is the other main newspaper on the island but more widely read in the south), order a *Cappuccino* and sit down for a read. OK, it's not so much of a read as a look at the pictures but informative nevertheless.

I'm just tucking into *Lo Sport* section when in walks Tommaso. He looks as though he's spent the whole night on the floor of a bar, been dragged through a hedge backwards and then, just for good measure, gone and done it all again. Red eyes, dishevelled hair and crumpled T-shirt complete the look and the heavy smell of cigarettes and booze confirms it. 'What the hell happened to you?' I say asking the bleeding obvious. He gestures to the barman and orders a *Caffè Corretto* (an espresso with a shot of brandy in it which I suppose does pretty much the same job as a Bloody Mary). 'A very good night my friend, a very good night' he manages in broken English. It transpires that after the Pizza the night before he'd gone off with some of the cast members and had a few too many *staffas* and then fallen off his proverbial horse. Maybe this isn't the time to bring up the technical minutia of theatre production as I think my friend is on the verge of bringing up something of his own. We agree to meet at 4pm at the rehearsal room and I leave Tommaso to nurse his hangover in peace. Apparently the *torno subito* sign is a permanent installation on his shop door.

With time to kill I decide to head off for a bit of little Britain and make my way to Licia's antique shop only five minutes away on Via Manno. Everything in Sassari is only five minutes away.

The sign outside reads *C'era Una Volta* (once upon a time) and unlike Tommaso's antique shop it's open. Licia is pleased to see me and excited about showing me her shop. It's only been open a year but she beams with pride as she ushers me through the door. Only about twenty square meters and stuffed with English antiques it is indeed little Britain. Licia doesn't specialise and the shop sells just about anything from old postcards and cricket bats to tables, wardrobes and dressers with a particularly large selection of Sheffield plate and assorted porcelain. There a small collection of jewellery which I'm told is not exactly legal, not that she's pinched it but she explains that in Italy you need a different sort of license to sell jewellery and it's very expensive to get one. It's something to do with insurance she tells me.

It's quite a surreal experience knowing that I'm on an island in the middle of the Mediterranean in thirty degree heat but surrounded by objects that are very obviously British. I grew up in a house full of antiques and there is something very comforting about Licia's shop where even the prints and paintings hanging on the walls are of typical English landscapes. A friend of mine once told me that you never actually own antiques but pay for the privilege of looking after them in your life time. Looking at the price of some of the stuff in Licia's shop I think I would rather own them. She's planning to open another shop next year she tells me so there is a market for the antiques she is selling. I'm pleased that she is doing so well with something she is obviously very passionate about.

I promise to pass by again soon and thank her for the guided tour. I leave comforted by the fact that 'There is some corner of a foreign field…'

It's 4.05pm when I arrive at the rehearsal room for my scheduled appointment with Tommaso. The door is already open and judging by the noise there is a hive of activity going on inside. Clean shaven with ironed shirt and pressed trousers Tommaso appears at the doorway. '*Sei in ritardo*' you're late he says. My defensive reply is drowned out by the sudden sound of rap music coming from within. A white man with dread locks, large sunglasses and head phones pokes his head around the door and introduces himself as Davide Merlini. *'Piacere sono Malachi'* (nice to meet you, I'm Malachi) I shout by way of reply. 'The best DJ in all of Sardinia' Tommaso proclaims above the din clapping Davide on the shoulder. He certainly does look the part and comes with his own costume. As if on cue two people arrive carrying a large costume rail full of clothes and proceed to muscle it through the doorway. Following close behind is a *ragazzo,* no more than eighteen years old with big baggy jeans, cap back to front and huge trainers (the type with the really large laces). Another with his own costume. I'm introduced to Roberto Chessa - the best break-dancer in all Sardinia. When I think about it I wouldn't have imagined that Italy could produce great break-dancers. Good food, fine wine, architecture, opera and much more but break-dancers? I want to put my completely unfounded prejudices aside and reserve judgment until a later time but it seems Roberto has other ideas. After a brief conversation with Mr Merlini the music changes and Roberto is off. Now I'm no expert on the intricate art of break-dancing but I do know one thing – if you can spin on your head that's pretty damn impressive. Not only can this guy spin on his head but he can do it without the support of his arms. Now that's genius. Italians can break-dance; he's going to be a show stopper. Most actors can dance a little, they have to learn it at drama school, but for something like this you have to call in the specialists. This isn't something they teach you at RADA. I look over at Tommaso who is grinning like a Cheshire cat, he knows I'm pleased. He tells me he has found all three cars and we can start costume fittings that evening. Any doubts I may have had about the show coming together are suddenly banished - at least for now.

The next person to arrive is Monica De Murtas, the Theatre critic from La Nuova Sardegna. Hmm…The Theatre critic from La Nuova Sardegna? - Tommaso forgot to tell me about that little one and apparently I have an interview with her now. I'm nervous again about being able to communicate properly in Italian but Tommaso assures me she does speak some English. We head over to a corner of the room for a bit of peace and quiet and pull up some chairs but our privacy is soon invaded. Driven by the possibility of immortality offered by a member of the press everyone else crowds into the corner to listen. Tommaso politely tells them '*va via*' and we settle down to the interview. Monica is very patient and makes sure I understand all the questions and that I'm happy with the answers I've given. It goes well and is all over in about ten minutes. She tells us the article should be out within a couple of days and will appear in the culture section of the newspaper. The paper has a circulation of approximately three hundred thousand so it was well worth doing and great publicity for the show. I have my photo taken (wishing I'd worn a cleaner shirt) and we say our goodbyes. I breathe a sigh of relief and think of cold beer.

After the evening session, by way of a change, we head to a *spaghetteria* called Sandrino on Viale Umberto on the edge of *il centro storico*. It's a fantastic place full of atmosphere and jam packed. My only regret is that we hadn't been here before. As well as some of the more well-known dishes such as *Carbonara* and *Pesto* the menu has almost every type of Spaghetti imaginable including: *Spaghetti Rana* (Spaghetti with frogs) and Spaghetti Whiskey which speaks for itself, but frogs!? The *Pelophylax kl. Esculentus*, or common European frog is an edible delicacy mostly found in the northern Italian lake district and is the same species that they eat in France. I also notice that they have a number of *penne* dishes on the menu one of the most popular being *Penne alla Vodka*. I decide to play it safe and go for the dish of the house *Spaghetti Sandro* made with oil, garlic, parsley, clams, mussels, fish roe, artichokes and fresh tomato. The portions are huge and absolutely delicious. The average price for a dish is a very reasonable six euros. Satisfied I walk the short distance home and to bed hoping not to meet Joe Pesci in my dreams.

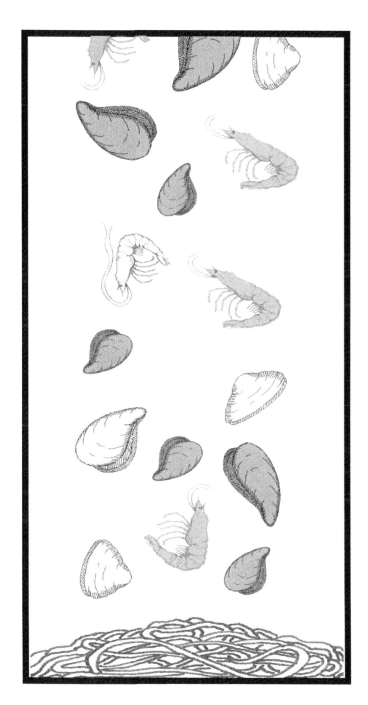

Spaghetti ai Frutti di Mare al Cartoccio

Serves 4

Ingredients

- 360g of spaghetti
- 350g of clams
- 350g of mussels
- 250g of prawns
- 200-300g of small calamari
- 4 ripe tomatoes
- 2 cloves of garlic
- basil
- parsley
- chilli pepper
- extra virgin olive oil
- salt
- pepper
- large glass of good quality dry white wine

Preparation

Soak the clams for three hours in salted cold water to remove the sand and impurities. Rinse every so often.

Clean and rinse the mussels thoroughly, remembering to remove the beards.

Thoroughly rinse the prawns under running water. Remove the antennae and legs that could come off while cooking and rinse again.

Clean the calamari and rinse them under running water and then cut into strips.

Plunge the tomatoes in boiling water for one minute, then peel and chop them into thin slices. Thinly slice the garlic and finely chop the parsley and basil.

Gently simmer half of the garlic in a pan with 2-3 tablespoons of olive oil, then add the chilli pepper, the mussels and clams and two thirds of the wine. Cover the pan and cook until all the shells are open. Remove the shells that might be empty and taste the sauce to make sure that no sand or grit is left.

In a separate big pan gently simmer the other half of the garlic with chilli pepper to taste and 1-2 spoons of olive oil. Add the calamari and the rest of the wine and cook for five minutes. Add the sliced tomatoes and salt and cook for 3 minutes, then add the prawns and cook for another 5 minutes. Add the contents of the first pan to the second.

In the meantime cook the spaghetti in boiling salted water and drain them "al dente". Pour them into the pan and add the parsley and basil. Mix and pour the contents of the pan, including the sauce, onto a large piece of foil.

Make a parcel with the foil and finish cooking in a pre-heated oven at 180 degrees for 5 minutes. Place the parcel on a serving dish and open. Enjoy.

***

This morning I'm meeting Marco Sanna to sign the contract for my new *Mansarda*. He has an office on Via Roma, north of Piazza Italia and we are due there at 11am. I swing by Little Britain to pick up Licia and we walk the short distance to number 54.

The sign on the bell says *Sanna Marco, Geometra* (surveyor). The office is on the first floor and waiting for us at the door is the man himself. In his mid-forties, slight and immaculately dressed Marco is a soft spoken Sardinian born here in the city and like most Sassaresi has spent his whole life here. In contrast his brother, he tells me, lives in London near Gloucester Road and teaches Karate.

The contract turns out to be quite straight forward: two months deposit, one month rent in advance, three months' notice if I want to leave and no pets. The rent will be due on the 1st of each month. I have to pay for the electricity and water that are both in Marco's name. If I want to transfer the utility bills to my name it will be too complicated he explains and apparently cost me more money as I'm not yet a resident.

Fine by me. The gas is bottled so I pay for that directly when it runs out and he gives me the number of the man who delivers it. If I want to put a telephone line in, again no problem but my expense. Licia checks the small print for any hidden extras and I willingly hand over one thousand and fifty euros in cash and sign on the dotted line. The sudden realisation that there is now no turning back gives me a moment of panic. I now have a responsibility, a commitment, an apartment I have rented and signed for in a foreign country. What have I done? Marco gives me a receipt and copy of the contract. I should be able to move in about two weeks but he will call to let me know the exact date. He wants to send in the cleaners first and give the whole place a lick of paint.

Before we leave he tells me his brother will be over next month and we should all go and get a coffee together. I'm not quite sure what I might have in common with Marco's brother except the fact that he lives in London. It certainly isn't Karate but agree to the coffee anyway.

The final week of rehearsals goes as planned with everything running to schedule. We're in good shape and despite everyone feeling a bit nervous there is a real sense of anticipation. The preview in the newspaper came out after a few days as promised and gave the whole cast a boost. It's a whole half page article with a big photo at the top and a headline screaming *DA NON PERDERE* (not to be missed). The excitement builds.

Technical rehearsals start the next morning at 8am in Teatro Verdi. I've lectured the cast on the absolute need for punctuality and made it clear that it's never too late to replace someone. OK this isn't entirely true but it seems to have the desired effect. For the theatrical novice here is a quick break down of how a two day technical rehearsal works.

Day 1

8am   *set, costumes and props arrive at the theatre.*

9am   *technicians hang the lights, in this case about 100.*

12am   *set goes onto the stage, borders and drapes are hung, floor gets put down.*

3pm   *lights are focused on stage.*

7pm   *lighting effects are plotted into a computer.*

11pm   *end.*

Day 2

8am   *sound check.*

9am   *cue to cue technical rehearsal with actors (entrances, exits, light cues, music cues, quick changes and scene changes).*

3pm   *dress rehearsal.*

9pm   *first performance.*

I would much prefer to start technical rehearsals with the actors at the end of day one but this depends on how smoothly things go in the morning. With forty people in the theatre including technicians, it is a real exercise in time management and coordination. If any one aspect of the process doesn't go according to plan it has a knock on effect on everything else. You could find yourself at 8pm on day two not having done a dress rehearsal. This is rare but working in an unknown Italian environment makes me apprehensive nonetheless. There are no previews here so everything hangs on the first performance, everything has to be perfect. In Italy it's traditional for the director to go on stage and take a bow at the end of the show with the cast but I think I'll make that call later. If the show goes badly I'll be leaving the theatre via the back door, giving three months' notice on my flat and skulking back to England with my tail between my legs.

Named after the famous nineteenth century romantic composer Teatro Giuseppe Verdi sits on the corner of Viale Umberto and Via Politeama. It's a barn of a place and with almost a thousand seats is the largest of the three main theatres in Sassari. Originally Victorian in design it was refurbished in the 1930's and now has a distinct air of imperialism about it. Despite its size the auditorium feels remarkably intimate and thankfully has great acoustics. (I have been worried about some of the less experienced actors not having enough voice to reach the back of the theatre and have, up until now, considered using microphones).

I arrive at 7.45am and to my relief almost everyone is on time. Tommaso, however, is nowhere to be seen. I really hope he didn't decide to go out last night and is still asleep on the floor of some bar or stuck halfway through a hedge.

I'm sitting in the stalls in the middle of explaining the schedule to the actors when Tommaso enters down stage right shouting '*Sono qui! Le macchine sono arrivate! Sono fuori! Venite, veloci veloci!*' – They're here! The cars have arrived, they're outside! Come, quickly, quickly! He exits as quickly as he entered. Everyone starts to get up and I have to tell them to remain seated until I've been to investigate. I leave the auditorium, cross the back of the stage, go down the nine meter concrete ramp where the cars will eventually come up, through a wide corridor and finally out through the dock doors of the theatre and into the street.

There in the middle of the road sits a forty foot, open top articulated lorry with three wrecked cars on the back. This would not usually be a problem but Viale Umberto is one of the main circular roads that run around Sassari – and it's rush hour. The road has two lanes and we're blocking one of them so it's imperative to off load the cars as quickly as possible.

The sound of blasting horns is already deafening. How did the cars get on the back of the lorry in the first place? I ask Tommaso. *'Una gru'* he replies. *'Una gru?'* I repeat not sure whether that's an answer or some sort of Neanderthal grunting. After a quick game of charades on the pavement I understand that he means 'a crane' (my first guess was 'a swan' which offended Tommaso as I had so obviously brought into question his skills as a mime). Well, there's no crane here now is there?! The technicians arrive and, immediately assessing the situation, decide to move fast and lift one of the cars off *veloce*. Even with six of them they are struggling and we all muck in, including the truck driver and try to get the first one off. After a lot of *vaffanculo*, *cazzo* and *pezzo di merda* we finally get it onto the pavement. A discussion ensues that sounds more like an almighty row but I know from experience that even when Italians talk about the weather it can sound like they're trying to kill each other. The only word I can make out is *motori* but everything becomes clear when they open the bonnet of the car to reveal the engine still in it. No wonder it's so bloody heavy. Never in a million years, let alone a couple of hours, will we get these cars up the concrete ramp and onto the stage.

News has obviously filtered through to the actors who start appearing one by one to see what's going on. There are now some thirty people on the street plus a load of angry motorists and the horn blasting is getting louder. This is a nightmare. And just when I though it couldn't get any worse the *Polizia Stradale* turn up. They demand that we move the lorry immediately or risk being towed, given a fine, being arrested or all three. It's decided that the truck driver will go off and wait somewhere until we are ready for the next car and in the meantime the technicians will take the engine out of the first one. Sounds like a good plan but they should be on the fucking stage rigging the fucking lights *cazzo*! I tell the actors to go back to the auditorium and start a line run while I head off to the dressing room to massage my temples and revise the schedule. It's going to be a long day.

The first car is on the ramp at 11am. Although relieved of its engine and wheels it's still incredibly heavy and takes fifteen people plus various ropes and dollies to manoeuvre it slowly up the concrete. Oil and petrol seem to leak from nowhere in particular further hampering the heroic efforts of everyone involved including a few of the actors. It's a piece of theatre in itself the likes of which you would never see in Britain. Apart from the oil and petrol, that would give even the most laid back dope smoking fire inspector a coronary, the fact that actors are risking injury by man-handling a couple of tons of rusted metal up a concrete ramp makes my insides churn - it's as if my stomach's playing host to a group of synchronised swimmers wearing clogs. A huge cheer accompanied by much hugging and back slapping hails the arrival of the first car on to the stage. One man's nightmare is another man's triumph. One down two to go.

Fortunately the first car was the only one with an engine so the other two are much quicker to unload. All three cars are on stage and in position by 1pm.

'Allora, andiamo a pranzo adesso, ci vediamo alle quattro va bene?'

This is Titti Sisto the chief technician (Titti is Italian for Tweety Pie, his real name is Antonio). I ask Tommaso for a translation.

'He says they are going to lunch now but they will be back at four is that OK?'

'No it's not OK! Why can't they have an hour for lunch like everybody else?' I snap trying to contain my anger.

'What, we only have an hour for lunch?' Tommaso complains.

One of the actors, overhearing the conversation decides to join in.

'Solo un'ora per pranzo?'

And then another,

'Un'ora per pranzo? Ma la mia mamma ha fatto Orata al forno'. Apparently his mother has cooked oven baked Bream.

I swear to god somebody is going to die in this theatre today but not before I get that fish recipe. Finally after much haggling the technicians agree to return at three. It's not ideal but I don't push it. I need to accept that working practices are different here and the last thing I want to do is piss off the technical crew. I agree to buy them all Ichnusa at the end of the day and this seems to go down well. A happy crew is a productive crew. The rest of the day goes relatively smoothly but we run out of time with the lighting plot. I decide to plot the rest of the states during the technical cue to cue the next morning. As promised I buy everyone a beer and thank them for their hard work. I head home for an early night. It's 1.30am.

Orata al forno

Serves 2

Ingredients

- *2 medium sized Bream (or similar) cleaned and gutted*
- *1kg salt*
- *1 lemon (quartered)*

Preparation

Cut two pieces of foil large enough to make separate parcels for the fish. On each piece spread 250g of salt patting gently until evenly spread and big enough to lay the fish on top. Place the fish on top of the salt and cover with the remaining salt again patting gently until the salt is relatively smooth and compact.

Close each parcel making sure the fish and salt are completely covered. Pre-heat the oven to 160 degrees. Place the fish parcels on a baking tray and cook for approximately 25 minutes.

When done gently open the parcels, break off the top layer of salt, lift the fish out and serve. Use the lemon to garnish.

Malachi Bogdanov

CHAPTER SIX

I'm in the theatre at 7.30am. Sound checking gets underway at 8am and by 9am we start the cue to cue with lights, music, full costume, set and props.

At the top of the show the actress playing Puck, Consuelo Pittalis, has to be set inside a fake grand piano as the audience are let into the auditorium half an hour before the scheduled start time. The problem is Puck doesn't make an entrance until the end of the first scene which is approximately twenty five minutes long which means Consuelo will be in the piano for almost an hour. If the show starts late, which is a distinct possibility in Italy, she could be in there for even longer. In rehearsals Consuelo insisted this wouldn't be a problem but the reality is very different. It's like being trapped in a small wooden box with no light for over an hour. Buried alive. On top of all this she is wearing full bondage gear, a black hockey mask and has to have a smoke machine and light in there with her for her entrance. It makes me nervous but the only way we'll know if she can do it or not will be in *la prova generale* (the dress rehearsal). We move quickly on.

Technical rehearsals can be very tedious with a lot of hanging around doing not a lot and it's a testament to the character of the Sardinians that they remain so calm and patient. Progress is slow and by lunch time we only have half the show completed. We are very behind. I brace myself for the 'how long do we have for lunch' discussion and, to the credit of the technicians, acknowledging that we are behind, they agree to take only an hour. I'll buy them more beer later. We finally finish at 5pm and will start *la prova generale* at 6pm. This will only give us an hour between the dress rehearsal and curtain up making it very tight with no margin for error. It's at this point that I know there is very little else I can do. It's now in the hands of the actors and technicians to deliver the show as rehearsed in accordance with the director's vision. I'm confident that the show is good but you never know exactly how it's going to go on the night. At 5.30pm we put Consuelo in the fake *piano forte* and wait the thirty minutes until 6pm. Precisely on the hour the run through starts and I sit nervously at the back of the stalls with pen, paper and torch waiting for Puck to enter. Twenty-five minutes later and exactly in time with the music the lid of the piano starts to rise. Lit only from within smoke spews slowly from the crack as first a hand, then an arm and then a face appear. Puck emerges almost in slow motion and takes the step down onto the waiting chair. It's a really great moment and I just want to hug Consuelo but remind myself that this is only a dress rehearsal and if there is any hugging to do it will be after the first performance. The rest of the run through goes pretty well with a lot of the usual errors associated with dress rehearsals. Most of the mistakes are mistakes that the actors and technicians know they have made and will clean up automatically. I'm more concerned with the ones they don't know they have made and with only ten minutes to give notes I have to make sure the notes count.

No sooner have we finished it's almost time to put Consuelo back in the Piano so I quickly call the actors on stage to wish them luck. Tommaso leads the Italian good luck ritual that turns out to be very different from the British version. We all have to stand in a circle while we softly chant *merda, merda, merda* and build slowly to a crescendo. When we reach a climax everybody breaks out of the circle and slaps each other on the arse! Now I can tell you once you've been slapped on the arse twenty five times it starts to sting a little and I consider watching the show standing up. It's certainly a far cry from the polite 'break a leg' scenario that we have in the UK and I make a note to find out where the ritual comes from and literally get to the bottom of it. Is it simply because the Italians want to imitate the French in order to give them a good hiding? I've since learnt that to 'break a leg' in Britain refers to sixteenth century actors kneeling down to pick up coins thrown by the audience, thus breaking the line of the leg. Of course the audience could equally throw rotten fruit and vegetables depending on what they thought of the performance. I hope this isn't the case tonight.

It's the moment of truth. Consuelo is in the piano, the audience is in the theatre and I'm in the bar. 9pm comes and goes and there is still a large queue for tickets at the box office and I start to worry about Consuelo. What if she passes out with the heat? What if she has a fit of claustrophobia? What if she simply nods off and misses her cue? I have this mental picture of the STP arriving and arresting me for unlawful imprisonment of a thespian.

The auditorium is full, almost a thousand people and at 9.30pm (half an hour late) we're ready to kick off. At the end of the first scene, after being inside the piano for an hour and twenty five minutes Consuelo finally emerges from captivity. I breathe a very big sigh of relief and head back to the bar. I'm too nervous to watch the rest of the show even though I do nip back and forth occasionally when I know there is a particularly difficult bit coming up. It appears to be going well with plenty of laughter and lots of applause at the end of scenes. I'm told that Italian audiences will let you know if they like or dislike something by booing or applauding so I'm relieved to hear it's the latter. I head back to the bar nevertheless and wait for the end.

The curtain comes down at 11.30pm to what I can hear is good applause. I make my way back stage deciding, with the help of a couple of beers, to face the public. The cast are now on their third bow and on seeing me in the wings gesture for me to come out. Maybe this is when the booing starts? Pins like jelly I walk the short distance to the centre of the stage and join them in a bit of 'leg-breaking'. A couple of bravos, no booing then the curtain closes and it's all over.

I start to relax and literally feel the tension slipping from my body as I slump onto the bonnet of one of the cars. Tommaso bounces up still energised by the experience and puts his arm around my shoulder – '*Tu hai fatto bene amico mio, tu hai fatto molto bene*' You did well my friend, you did very well. He says. Everyone joins in the obligatory kissing, back slapping and hugging that make up the mutual admiration society that always exists after a first night. Suddenly the wings are full of people I've never met before. Grannies, granddads, godmothers, godfathers, uncles, aunts, cousins, husbands, wives, girlfriends, boyfriends, fiancés, sons, daughters, granddaughters, grandsons, mums, dads, friends, friends of friends (and I'm sure a pet or two) crowd onto the stage congratulating the actors. It's like a wedding. The actors are still in their costumes and the stage is strewn with cables, lights, props and bits of set - an accident waiting to happen. Things certainly are different here. I head for the safety of *il camerino* (the dressing room) for a well-deserved smoke on the balcony.

Halfway through my Camel Tommaso comes in carrying a metal box and proceeds to count out money on the table. He takes out an envelope, stuffs in a bundle of cash and hands it to me. *'Grazie mille'* he says. I was told that I would be paid after the first performance but I didn't expect it to be ten minutes after the first performance and in cash. You've got to love this country. It's not a huge amount of money but more than you would like to carry around in your wallet. It wouldn't fit to start with. Tommaso has obviously been to the box office for the takings so none of it is in large denominations – a proper wad. I gladly take *i soldi* but refrain from counting it in front of him. When I first took the job he said *'la mia parola è il mio contratto'* (my word is my contract) so not wanting to offend him I decide to count it later knowing full well that if it's short there is nothing I can do about it. I make the excuse that I need *il bagno* and quickly head off to the bathroom to check my wad.

People say that Italy has a large cash economy because the taxes are so high. The government knows that people deal in cash so keep the taxes deliberately high and because they remain deliberately high people continue to deal in cash. I'm not sure how accurate this circular analogy is but it would certainly explain a lot. Satisfied that it's all there I put the cash conspicuously into my front pocket, flush the toilet and furtively head out into the foyer. I feel like I've just done a drug deal or at least just sold Shakespearian direction on the theatrical *Mercato Nero*.

When I finally arrive the Pizzeria is packed. There must be at least fifty people at two extremely long tables. As I enter there is an eruption of applause and Tommaso shows me to my seat at the head of one of the tables. It makes me feel good. I'm pleased we've managed to produce a show that's obviously a new departure for Sassari and hope that the company can move forward with the momentum and continue to create exciting work. Especially prose which there seems to be a distinct lack of.

The festivities continue well into the night. I think it's a huge relief as well as a huge experience for everyone involved, myself included and nobody can blame them for soaking up every last drop of the moment. I can hardly keep my eyes open but go through the party motions knowing that tomorrow morning there's nothing to get up for.

It's what I call post show blues. After working so intensely for a month surrounded by people and always on the move suddenly there's nothing. My job is done. No more rehearsals, no more, meetings, no more fun. Just emptiness. I've always considered myself lucky getting paid for something I love doing and never thought of it as work. It really is what I live for so when it comes to an end it takes me three or four days to come out of the depression before I can look forward to the next job. This time the feeling is compounded by the fact that I have changed my life at the same time and find myself in a foreign country with only the seeds of a new beginning and no more work. The reality of the situation makes me home sick but I know the feeling is momentary. Licia calls - things are looking up.

AGLIO

CHAPTER SEVEN

They call it 'the road of death'. It's the SS597 and runs 100km from just south of Sassari all the way to Olbia and the Golfo Aranci in the north east. In the last five years alone it has claimed the lives of over forty people with most of these deaths being attributed to bad driving. The road is so infamous it now has its own campaign group, *Strada Olbia Sassari* (S.O.S) and its own website. Apparently there was 470 million euros ear-marked for its reconstruction to a four lane motorway but the money mysteriously disappeared.

We take the SS131 and then the turning for Olbia and onto *La Strada della Morte*! Dun dun dun! It looks like any other road to me but you can imagine drivers late at night, wanting to get home quickly, risking a bit of overtaking on its many curves. Every so often we pass a bunch of flowers on the road side, a grim reminder of the lives it's claimed. Fortunately we are only on it for a short distance and after twenty kilometres turn off for Tempio Pausania on the SS127. Our destination is L'Agnata di De André the former home of the late singer, songwriter and poet Fabrizio De André whose farmstead is now open to the public for Agritourism.

Born in 1940 in Genoa, De André rose to fame with his songs and poems about marginalized and rebellious people, above all prostitutes, who were seen by De André as the answer to bourgeois prissiness. In 1979 he was kidnapped by Sardinian bandits and held prisoner in the Supramonte Mountains in the centre of the island. He was released four months later after the ransom was reportedly paid. When his captors were eventually apprehended by the police, De André was called as witness before the Court. He showed compassion for some of his kidnappers, since he was well treated by what he called 'guardians' and declared his own solidarity with them - 'They were the real prisoners, not I'.

He died of cancer in 1999 and is remembered as a real people's poet, a champion of the ordinary man and is often compared to Bob Dylan.

Kidnapping tourists has long been a quaint rural occupation in Sardinia and on my first visit back in 1991 I was advised not to take a taxi in any of the central parts of the island. Licia tells me it was a 'past time' and rarely happens today. I put the word 'rarely' out of my mind and continue along this remote, isolated, mountain road miles from anywhere.

The SS127 spirals up though lush, beautiful Cork Oak foliage in the direction of Tempio. Cork trees are stripped of their precious natural material entirely without machinery and appear almost naked from the waist down. Cork Oak can live for up to 250 years and Virgin cork, or 'male' cork, is the first cork cut from trees approximately twenty-five years old. Another ten to fifteen years of maturation is required for the second harvest and a tree can be harvested up to a dozen times in its life. The *sughero* industry in Europe produces a staggering 340,000 tons of cork a year, fifty percent of which comes from Portugal. Its estimated value is a whopping 1.5 billion euros with a work force of 30,000 people. Wine corks constitute 15% of cork usage by weight but 66% of revenues. This means that 51,000 tons of cork goes towards bottling our wine at a cost of 99 million euros. I check for bandits, get out of the Punto and nick some cork. I'm in the wrong business.

We eventually pass though the historic town of Tempio and head south into the heart of Gallura. Up until 1410 Sardinia was divided into four provinces: Logudoro in the north west, Cagliari in the south, Arborea in the west and Gallura (meaning rooster or cock from the Latin *Gallus*) in the north east. These were the original indigenous Kingdoms of the island known as Giudicati, each with its own separate *giudice* or Judge. Gallura is now absorbed into the new region of Olbia/Tempio but the local population still prefers to call themselves Galluresi – cocks!

About five kilometers south of Tempio we make a right turn at a sign for L'Agnata and follow what is first a road and then a track deep into luscious forest. For what seems like an eternity we bump down this narrow tree lined tunnel until we finally come to another sign saying 'Agritourism'. We drive up a small incline and park in a designated parking area for residents.

The place is idyllic. Covered by a canopy of grapevines a grass walkway takes us past a lake on our right, a vegetable garden on our left and finally up to the house. Completely covered with Canadian Ivy, sitting in its own natural amphitheater, surrounded by fruit trees is the double-fronted granite farmhouse. I decide immediately that I want to live here (and that's before I see the swimming pool (cut out of natural rock), taste the food and sample the wine. It really is a small piece of paradise miles from anywhere in the most beautiful setting and we're here for two days.

We check-in at reception and are shown to our room. Behind the main building is a newer construction built in the 80's with eight ensuite double bedrooms. Covered with the same Canadian Ivy it blends in effortlessly with the house and garden and has excellent views over the pool and surrounding woodland. Furnished with simple drapes, cushions and reproduction wooden furniture the room is clean, cosy and quiet – the perfect retreat. I ignore the Minibar in the corner knowing from experience that this innocent little fridge is more than capable of getting the better of me and doubling my bill for the weekend. Nasty little temptress.

Dinner is served at 8pm so more than enough time for a dip in the pool, some mindless fiction and a little nap in the shade.

By five o'clock I'm gasping for a drink. The little white siren beckons from within luring my credit card to certain death on the icy rocks of a gin and tonic. Licia tries in vain to pull me back but I'm weak and the fridge is too strong. I can't resist the lure of its sweet melodic humming drawing me closer and closer. I desperately try to escape but it's no good, I'm trapped in my own personal Odyssey with no way out. Exhausted and thirsty I'm finally lost to that ruin of many a poor boy – the Minibar. I tell myself I'm just going to have the one but hey, who am I kidding. I resign myself to the inevitable and go in search of a lemon.

Having found the indispensable fruit on a nearby tree I settle down to my aperitif by the pool. Licia joins me with an orange juice and we savor the costly moment watching the sun go down over the deep green mountains accompanied by the soft symphony of crickets. Romantic bliss.

It's 7.45pm and we're waiting outside the main entrance to the house to be ushered in for dinner. There must be twenty-five people waiting to go in, certainly more people than there are beds. Providing there is enough room you can book a table just like a restaurant but the resident guests will always get priority. As with Sa Mandra the menu is fixed so you eat what you are given and, as we know, to avoid any confrontation, eat as much as you can. The problem is I know from experience there's going to be mountains of it.

At 8pm sharp a waiter appears and takes us through the house and into a large dining room to the rear. A huge window runs the full length of the wall giving a generous view of the garden at the back and the pool beyond. Carafes of wine, red and white, sit patiently on the tables together with a large selection of appetizers including *prosciutto crudo, formaggio, olive* and *cipolle sottoaceto.* I do like a good pickled onion and they do sound tastier in Italian and somehow more refined. The Italian language can tempt you to eat all kinds of things you wouldn't otherwise consider putting in your mouth. *Uova sottoaceto* for example sounds infinitely more palatable than 'pickled egg' and you might just be tempted to have one. I explain my theory to Licia and she agrees but points out that however well dressed in vernacular there are certain dishes you would never voluntarily put in your gob – *Pisello di Pecora* being one - Sheep's dick! I think she has a point.

With my appetite well and truly quelled in comes the *primi piatti*. I won't take you through all the courses but there are a few that absolutely deserve a mention. The first is *Ravioli di cinghiale con sugo di noci* (wild boar ravioli with walnut sauce), more like foreplay to the main event but absolutely delicious nevertheless. The second is *Zuppa Gallurese* which is quite simply one of the tastiest dishes I have ever eaten. Sex on a plate it is.

Ravioli di cinghiale con sugo di noci

Serves 4 (NB. the prep time is a lengthy business)
Ingredients
- *500g flour*
- *4 eggs*
- *1 onion (finely chopped)*
- *1 stick of celery (chopped)*
- *1 carrot (chopped)*
- *salt*
- *olive oil*
- *500g of wild boar (if you can't get wild boar you can use high quality domestic pork)*

- *litre red wine*
- *parmesan*

For the sauce

- *½ cup olive oil*
- *250g walnuts*
- *clove of garlic*
- *30g pine nuts*
- *40g parmesan*
- *250ml milk*
- *1 sprig marjoram*
- *40g bread crumbs*
- *salt*

Prepare the meat - Put the wild boar in a bowl with cold water and rest for an hour before rinsing thoroughly in running water. Repeat the above process 3-4 times.

Chop half an onion, half a carrot and half a stick of celery and place in a bowl with the meat. Add a bay leaf, a leaf of sage, a small sprig of rosemary and a clove of garlic. Cover with red wine and rest for 6 hours. Rinse the meat and throw everything else away. Repeat the above resting the meat for another 6 hours.

Preparation

Spread a little flour on a table. Put a little bit of olive oil on your hands so that the flour doesn't stick.

Mix the 500g of flour with a glass of warm water (added slowly) and work the mixture until you get a soft, elastic dough. Add a bit more water if necessary. Make the dough into a ball. Cover it with a cloth for half an hour and then start working on the ball again until the dough is smooth and soft. Divide the dough in half and using a rolling pin make two large rectangles approximately 3mm thick.

The filling - In a pan fry the onion, celery and carrot in a little olive oil until soft and then add the wild boar and cook on a low heat for about two hours. Once cooked let it cool and cut into small chunks.

Put the chunks in a blender with an egg and a handful of parmesan cheese. Blend the ingredients until the mixture is as smooth as possible.

Divide the dough in half and using a rolling pin make two large rectangles approximately 3mm thick.

Take a teaspoon and put separate blobs of mixture on to one of the pasta rectangles at regular intervals.

Cover with the second rectangle of pasta and gently push the pasta with your fingers between one bit of ricotta and another. Separate the ravioli using a cutter or simply a small glass. Cook in boiling water for approximately 3 minutes.

The Sauce - Boil the walnuts for 5 minutes so that they are easier to peel. Drain and let them cool. Meanwhile, put the bread in a bowl with the milk and when soggy, squeeze out the milk from the bread and set both aside.

Peel the walnuts and put them in a blender along with the pine nuts, garlic, parmesan and oil.

Add the bread and the marjoram. Add the milk from the squeezed bread and blend all the ingredients together until you have a thick creamy paste. Salt to taste.

Transfer to a pan and heat through. After draining the ravioli add them to the pan with the sauce and mix until the pasta is completely covered. Add freshly ground black pepper and drizzle with olive oil.

Zuppa Gallurese

Serves 4

Ingredients:

- *casareccio bread (or focaccia)*
- *300g pecorino cheese*
- *300g peretta cheese (or gruyere or gouda)*
- *300g grated parmesan*

- *1/4 cup chopped Italian parsley*
- *black pepper*
- *lamb broth*

For the broth

- *350g lamb*
- *350g beef*
- *1 onion, peeled and studded with 1 whole clove*
- *1 carrot, peeled*
- *1/2 cup celery leaves*
- *1/2 cup parsley stems*
- *1 clove of garlic*
- *1 teaspoon salt*
- *8 whole black peppercorns*

Preparation

Place the lamb/beef in a stockpot. Pour in 12 cups of cold water or enough to cover. Bring to the boil and skim off froth. Add remaining ingredients and simmer, partially covered, over low heat for 2 hours. Strain the broth through a fine sieve, discarding the meat and vegetables. Let cool. Chill and skim off fat.

Cut the bread into 2cm slices. Cut half of the peretta into slices and grate the remainder and the other cheeses into separate bowls. Chop the parsley and add to the freshly grated parmesan. Add black pepper to taste.

Bring the broth to a boil. Place the slices of bread on the bottom of an oven proof dish. Sprinkle a generous amount of pecorino over the bread and then a generous amount of the parmesan and then peretta. Repeat for a second layer – bread, pecorino, parmesan, peretta. Add another layer of bread.

Ladle the hot broth over the bread and cheese until it is all wet but not soggy. Put the remaining slices of peretta on top.

Bake in a pre-heated oven at 180 degrees for about 30 minutes or until the peretta is brown on top. Take out of the oven and let sit for 5 minutes then tuck in to this wonderfully delicious dish.

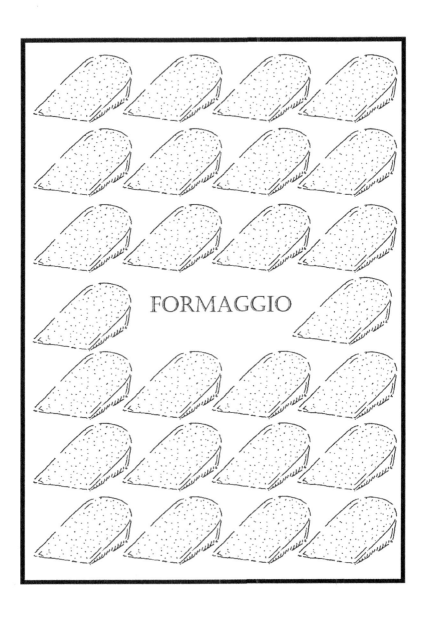

Last but not least is the dessert. This is the cigarette course, the winding down after the bout of passionate culinary love making with the *Zuppa Gallurese*. I settle for a lemon sorbet.

'Food has replaced sex in my life, now I can't even get into my own pants' someone anonymous once said. I hope the feeling is only temporary.

We head out into the warm September night to round off the evening with a *digestivo* under the stars. The waiter arrives and we both order Mirto Rosso. He comes back immediately with two glasses and the bottle that he promptly leaves on the table - always a mistake.

Mirto Rosso or Mirto Bianco is Sardinia's national liqueur and is made by emaciating fresh red or white berries from the Myrtle tree in alcohol. (I have to boast that I have had the good fortune to visit the oldest white berry Myrtle tree in the world which is actually in Agrigento, Sicily near the Valley of Temples). It's not the lightest of digestives but totally drinkable all the same. We make a good job of the bottle and decide to call it a night. We thank the waiter (who gives us a look that says 'I hope we have another bottle of Mirto because maybe some of the other guests would like some') and retire to our room. I avoid eye contact with the Minibar and head to bed.

The following day is more of the same (lying by the pool, reading pulp fiction, raiding the Minibar etc.) but it does give me a chance for a bit of quiet reflection.

It's now two weeks since I finished A Midsummer Night's Dream and there are a few positive signs of more work on the horizon. Pier Paolo Conconi, the artistic director of one of the state subsidized companies, came to see the show and was impressed. He has asked me if I would like to direct Alice in Wonderland for his company, La Botte e il Cilindro next Christmas. It's good work with a recognized company and I accept but it is a little way off. I really need something now. I have an offer to direct Pinocchio in Birmingham in November and it looks like I'm going to have to do it just to survive. It's only four weeks work and means I can get through the next few months. Sardinia to Birmingham is a huge cultural leap but at least the company of Pinocchio will be Italian if not a little wooden. Tommaso wants to do Romeo and Juliet next but that won't happen until the spring and in the meantime he has promised to organize some workshop/seminars just to keep *il lupo* from the door.

I move into the new *mansarda* next week so hopefully that will make me feel a little less transient and give me some proper focus. I have the keys and should be in on Wednesday. Things with Licia seem to be going well. It's early days but there is nothing like a bit of romance to keep the spirits up.

Joking aside, with Licia it feels very natural, undemanding and open – I suppose the way it always should. It's more of an instant attraction and less 'When Harry met Sally', or in Italian '*Harry ti presento Sally*', which is a good thing as I don't think the famous 'Meg Ryan faking an orgasm in the restaurant scene' would go down too well here in L'Agnata. For those of you that don't remember the scene the dubbed version goes something like this: *'Oh...Oh Dio...Ooo Oh Mio Dio...Oh...Oh...Oh...Oh Dio...Oh Si Ecco Lo Oh! Oh... Sì Sì Sì Sì Sì Sì...Oh...Oh...Sì Sì Sì....Oh...Sì Sì Sì Sì Sì Sì...Oh...Oh... Oh... Oh Mio Dio Oh... Oh... Huh...'*
But as I said - early days.

8pm comes around far too quickly and it's off to the dining room for another marathon sitting followed by the other half of the Mirto bottle and a Limoncello on the terrace.

The next morning it's back to Sassari and reality and we make our way to reception to assess the damage. Full board is a hundred euros a night per person which I think is very reasonable given the location and quality of the food. The Minibar however is a disproportionate thirty-five euros but what the hell. Four hundred and thirty-five euros lighter we head for the Punto and back to the smoke via a little cork stealing on the way. It's a fabulous place and we make a pact to come back soon.

LIMONCELLO

CHAPTER EIGHT

The door is open when I arrive at number 15 Via Largo Infermeria San Pietro and the distinct smell of paint wafts from within. I'm supposed to move in today and have all my worldly possessions in the car ready and waiting in the street below but it appears the decorators have yet to finish. I say decorators but it's one bloke with a paint brush and a tin of watered down emulsion.

He puts down his bottle of Ichnusa and shakes my hand introducing himself as Mario and says he's working as fast as he can to get the place finished. I decline the offer of a swig and ask him if I can give him *una mano* to speed things up a bit. Unfortunately there is only one paint brush and I have to endure the spectacle of not so Super Mario leisurely whitewashing the apartment. It's taking forever. Is he being paid by the hour or what? I decide to start bringing stuff up from the car anyway. Before I know it it's one o'clock and Mario announces he's off to lunch and will be back at five. I was prepared for this and see it as an opportunity rather than a delay. As long as he doesn't take his *tinta e pennello* with him for a bit of lunchtime moonlighting I can probably finish the job by the time he gets back.

At 5.10pm I'm done and twenty minutes later Mario eventually turns up. He looks around the flat and nods approvingly knowing that he's just been paid for having a large bowl of pasta, a glass of wine and a nap. I'm happy if he's happy.

We start a little light chatting and the conversation finally comes around to 'So, what's an Englishman like you doing in Sassari?' I tell him what I do for a living and that I've just directed a Midsummer Night's Dream at Teatro Verdi. It transpires that his wife is a very keen Shakespeare fan and went to see my show. What are the chances? Mario is very excited and insists on calling his wife so I can say hello to her. I take the *telefonino* reluctantly, not quite sure how the conversation is going to go, but thankfully she does most of the talking leaving me free to grimace enthusiastically at Mario. She insists I come round for some seasonal *Ricci* (whatever they are) in the near future and makes me promise to exchange telephone numbers with her husband before he leaves. Life is full of surprises.

I swap numbers with Mario before a firm hand shake, a big hug, a kiss on both cheeks and finally an *arrivederci*. It turns out that Mario really is 'Super'.

It takes me the best part of the evening to carry the rest of my stuff up the four flights of stairs and put it into some kind of order and I'm starting to tire. Not wanting to move another inch I get pizza and beer delivered from a local pizzeria called *Bruno* and sit and contemplate my new home. I'm in at last. This is my flat, my life and my new beginning. But how long will it last? How long will I be here for? What does the future hold?

I find some sheets, throw them on the bed and using a pile of clothes as a pillow crash out immediately, utterly exhausted and high on paint fumes.

Ricci - Sea urchins are a delicacy in Sardinia. Between January and March you can buy them at most of the fishermen's stalls on the beach in Alghero and they appear on restaurant menus as the popular *Spaghetti ai Ricci di Mare*. I like to eat them raw straight from the shell with a teaspoon! If you like seafood, then sea urchins are the best you can have. The taste is unmistakable. It's a perfect balance between the sweet taste of seafood and the salty taste of the sea.

There are strict rules governing the time of year, the daily amount and the size of the urchins which can be fished and these regulations vary from region to region. In Sardinia it is possible to catch them from the 1st November through to the 4th May, but there is a daily limit of 50 sea urchins and the size is regulated. Sea urchins must be at least 7cm in diameter including the spikes.

RICCI

Spaghetti ai Ricci di Mare

Serves 4

Ingredients

- *400-450g of spaghetti*
- *20 sea urchins*
- *1 clove of garlic*
- *parsley*
- *extra virgin olive oil*
- *1 red chilli*

Preparation

Cut open the sea urchin shells and using a teaspoon remove and set aside the orange fleshy interior.

Boil the spaghetti in plenty of salty water. Fry the garlic and chilli in extra virgin olive oil. Chop the parsley and drain the pasta. Keep a cup of water to add in when mixing with the oil, chilli and garlic.

Put the spaghetti in the oil with the garlic, add the sea urchins and mix. The heat from the pan will melt the sea urchins giving a smooth consistency. Add fresh parsley and serve.

Today is *Permesso di Soggiorno* day. If you want to stay in Italy legally you need to have a permit even if you are an EU citizen. Technically I should have done this when I arrived but never got round to it.

I have to go to a place called l'Ufficio Stranieri (the office for foreign people) on Via Diego Murgia to the north of the old town. Despite my paint fumes hangover I wake up early wanting to be there ahead of any queues and to make sure I can find somewhere to park. As I imagined the building is a pretty ugly sixties construction, a big block of concrete on the outside and government issue municipal grey on the inside. I'd been told that the office opens at 9am so I arrive at 8.45am only to be told that it's shut on Thursdays and I have to come back on a Monday, Wednesday or Friday. Typical!

At 1pm I pick up Licia at Little Britain and head towards the suburb of Sassari called Buddi Buddi for lunch with her parents. Buddi Buddi is on the road to Platamona and takes about fifteen minutes in the car. We make a right turn off the main road and follow a small winding lane for about a kilometre before arriving at a large metal double gate.

What Licia hasn't told me is that her parents have three dogs and there, barking uncontrollably behind the *cancello,* are two Rottweiler's and an Alsatian and they mean business. Fuck. A three headed, twelve legged snarling monster! I hate dogs. (When I was a kid I was bitten by an Alsatian - in Italy of all places). Licia assures me they are just being playful. Yeah, right. She gets out of the car and opens the gate and they're immediately up on their hind legs licking her face. *'Ciao cuccioli miei'* 'Hello my little puppies' she says. Puppies? They're bigger than she is for Christ's sake! I wind up the window and drive through the gate. Licia gets back in the car and we continue down a narrow track with the monster in hot pursuit. I feel a bit sick.

The house has two hectares of land filled with olive trees which Licia tells me give the family enough oil for about a year. As we reach the end of the track I become aware of a clacking sound coming from the *alberi*. Licia's dad is standing under one of the trees with some sort of electric contraption designed to dislodge the olives. On closer inspection it looks like a long pole with two plastic rake heads facing each other that beat furiously together to dislodge the fruit. I definitely want to have a go on that later. Spread out on the ground are large green nets that catch the falling *olive* making them easier to collect later.

It's time to get out of the car. Seeing the complete look of terror on my face Licia gets out first and locks the dogs in a small pen in one corner of the garden. She must think I'm a real English wimp but you should see the size of these bad boys – they're no puppies.

I'm introduced to Franco, a man in his late forties, early fifties and a real charmer. The only problem is I can't understand a word he says. He has a strange accent that I've never heard before but I'm sure he says the same about me. We go into the house and I meet Adele, Lucia's mum. She's a little younger than Franco and the spitting image of her daughter. We're eating *agnello* for lunch and there on the table nestling among the roast potatoes is a whole lamb. In Italy they slaughter their lamb when it's only a few weeks old so the sight of this tiny creature in its entirety is literally a little hard for me to swallow. When you have a leg or a shoulder you never envisage the rest of the animal but little imagination is needed to see this little Snowy bouncing around a spring meadow. It does, however, smell divine.

Franco comes in with a bottle of local wine and we sit down for a little pasta before tucking into the meat. Franco and Adele are market traders or *ambulanti* as they are called in Italian. They do six markets a week getting up at four in the morning to sell a whole array of kitchen utensils. I can't help thinking it must be a hard life but they look good on it. At least they don't have to get up in freezing temperatures and brave the cold for ten hours a day like they do in the UK.

With the pasta finished it's time for Snowy. Just as I'm wondering how you carve a small baby lamb Franco supplies the answer. From a draw in the kitchen he takes out a pair of garden pruning shears and proceeds to cut up the lamb into large chunks. It is positively medieval. I can't help thinking how disapproving my mother would be of this obvious display of masculine, carnal butchery. Being so young the meat is almost white and slightly resembles chicken, very different from British lamb that's much darker and probably comes from New Zealand anyway. It's extremely tasty and I have to admit that it's the first time I have had a whole leg to myself, in fact we each have a leg! I tell them about mint sauce and they think it's an odd thing to eat with lamb. Here they generally like their roast served straight up, no sauce no gravy just potatoes. Vegetables come later in the form of raw carrots, celery and fennel to help digestion. We round off lunch with a homemade *Biancomangiare* and a Mirto. Excellent.

Biancomangiare

Serves 6-8

Ingredients

- *1 litre of milk*
- *200g of sugar*
- *100g corn starch*
- *1 lemon*

Preparation

Dissolve the corn starch in a cup of milk. In a pan gently heat and stir the rest of the milk, the sugar and lemon zest (peeled but not grated yellow skin of the lemon). Add the corn starch and milk mixture to the pan and keep heating on a gentle flame while stirring. Continue until the mixture becomes dense. Remove from the heat and take out the lemon zest. Pour into wet moulds (cupcake size and splashed with cold water). Leave to cool down and serve.

***

Living in Italy it's very difficult not to talk about food. Of course everyone has to eat but there's eating and there's eating. In Italy it's not only a way of surviving - it's a job, a pastime, a hobby, a sport, an art, a vocation, a craft, a craze, a distraction, a diversion, a fancy, an occupation, a game, an interest, a leisure activity, a leisure pursuit, an obsession, a topic, a quest, a relaxation, a side-line, a specialty, a weakness, a whim and something that cannot be ignored.

I thank Franco and Adele for a superb lunch and leave them watching a dubbed version of 'The Bold and the Beautiful' (apparently something they watch religiously every day). The three headed monster is still in its kennel when we make our way to the car - but it's staring at me.

LIMONE

CHAPTER NINE

It's now November and with Carlo Collodi in hand I'm heading back to Blighty to recharge the bank account. I'm not particularly looking forward to going back, it feels like I have to put my Italian life on hold just as it's gathering momentum. Tommaso has secured some funding for me to direct an outdoor version of The Nativity at Christmas and although I'm very grateful I have to say that it wouldn't be my first choice of play. He assures me I can direct an alternative version and not worry about offending the religious community. He promises they'll get the irony. I'll start as soon as I return.

The trip back does give me the chance to stock up on a few British fundamentals that I can't seem to live without. A box of ten aspirin costs 3.95 euros in Sardinia. An exorbitant amount compared to the UK. When the Italians want to refer to something that is very expensive they say it's a *farmacia* and I can see why. Try as I might I can't seem to find bacon in Sassari. There are lots of different types of wonderful *pancetta* but nothing that tastes quite the same as a bit of good old smokey. Maybe in time I'll wean myself off it as my palette becomes more Mediterranean? Oxo cubes. I have to buy Oxo cubes. Even the Italians use ready-made stock and it's a romantic misconception to think they are all up at the crack of dawn making beef or chicken broth. There's nothing wrong with Oxo cubes, nothing I tell you!

I say goodbye to my new life in the sun and make the short trip to Alghero airport and on to Stansted.

It's 7am on a cold Saturday morning in November, driving rain and wind bite at my jacket as I stand on the runway of a disused airfield in the middle of Nottinghamshire. This is the old Second World War air force base at Winthrop outside Newark and home to the bi-monthly Newark antiques fair. Knowing that Licia was off to buy merchandise during my stay in Birmingham I couldn't pass up the opportunity to see where all those British antiques get bought and shipped off to warmer climes. Stalls and marquees stretch along the weathered tarmac as far as the eye can see selling every antiquity imaginable from ships' compasses to teddy bears – a real dealer's Mecca.

At one end of the strip, set back from the stalls, is a huge grass car park playing host to every conceivable mode of goods transportation. Tens of articulated lorries form an ominous backdrop, their gaping doors wide open ready to gorge themselves on the mass of antiques only to be regurgitated on some foreign shore. Belgium, France, Germany, Italy, Holland, Argentina and even Japan are just a few of the dozens of countries represented, all hungry for a bit of Britain. It's an exodus.

Licia introduces me to the other Italian dealers, who, despite the weather, wrestle with bubble wrap to protect their precious cargo. Their lorry is only half full but already seems to contain a colossal amount of stuff. Another dealer arrives called Giorgio and parks up next to the artic in a rented Ford transit. He opens the doors of the van and calls for help unloading three up-right pianos. Who buys this stuff in Sardinia? I've been into a few houses now on the island and nobody has a bloody piano let alone a British one.

Where do all these antiques come from? This fair happens six times a year, year in year out and is one of many in Britain. It's surprising we have any antiques left at all! A decade from now they will be at a premium in the UK as most of them will have been shipped abroad.

I button up my coat and think about opening a shop if I ever return to this wet and windy island.

I'm back home at the beginning of December and excited about continuing my new life in Sassari. Christmas is well on its way, Nativity rehearsals begin tomorrow and I can't wait to get started.

The first thing I notice is how cold it is. Unlike the grey depressing winters in Britain the sky is electric blue but there is a distinct nip in the air especially in my apartment. Most of the old buildings don't have central heating so people are reliant on portable heaters or log fires. I immediately decide to find some logs and test my *camino*. I get out my dictionary and find the word for wood, *legno* and flip through the *pagine gialle* (yellow pages) for a supplier. There's one on the edge of town on the road to Porto Torres about ten minutes away.

I arrive at what I presume is the place judging by the huge piles of logs outside and park up next to a small hut. A short, bald, oval shaped man emerges from the cabin and asks what I want – '*cosa vuoi?*' I would have thought that was bloody obvious, it's not as if he's got kitchen units sitting outside. '*Legno*' I reply. '*Umm*' he says looking around as if he doesn't know where he's put it. We could not be surrounded by more wood. He eventually looks at my Punto and then back at one of the larger piles of logs apparently calculating the mass verses volume equation. He gestures for me to open the boot and proceeds to throw wood onto an ancient pair of iron scales (I wonder if they're English?). When the scales are balanced he starts to fill the Punto. '*Un quintale di olivo va bene?*' he says. I understand that it's olive wood but don't know what *quintale* means. As long as it fills the boot it should be enough to be getting on with (I find out later that *quintale* means 100kg which is certainly what it feels like as I carry it up my four flights of stairs). He finishes loading and for good measure throws in an extra log – '*È Natale*' he says and starts laughing uncontrollably. It's Christmas. I hand over fourteen euros and jump in the car. As I drive off I can still see him laughing in the rear view mirror. Crazy old Sard!

It's 5pm and I decide to head into town to soak up a bit of Italian Christmas atmosphere before going home to *accendere il camino*. The main drag is awash with Christmas lights as are all the shops, statues and municipal buildings. The sweet smell of roasting chestnuts hangs in the air and the sound of a brass band piping out Christmas carols completes the seasonal picture. Why do they always seem to do Christmas better on the continent? Everything is so tasteful. I remember having Christmas in London once and all the city centre lights had been sponsored by Birds Eye. All along Bond Street, Oxford Street and Regent Street you had these garish, tacky lights advertising frozen food. Tourists coming to London for the first time must have thought that we didn't have Santa Claus in Britain but Captain Birds Eye instead. I can see the similarities.

If you go into an Italian shop at Christmas they will happily wrap the items for you for free. In the UK they will wrap them but begrudgingly and more often than not for a small fee.

I head up to Piazza Azuni where we'll be doing the show in ten days' time and duck into Coffee Break for a glass of Cannonau. It doesn't sound like a very Italian bar but it does have a good selection of wine and excellent food (all you can eat buffet for 8 euros).

Cannonau is a dry, red wine produced right across the island in large quantities mainly concentrated in the central areas. Its ruby red colour varies in intensity depending on the region or year and as the wine gets older it takes on a slightly orange hue. A Sommelier would say it contains the faint aromas of cherry and mint but to be honest I couldn't tell the difference. Most Sardinians drink Cannonau with traditional meat dishes such as suckling pig, lamb and even goat. It is Sardinia's most popular wine and some argue the Mediterranean's oldest. Even though most of the experts believe that it comes from Iberia recent study has proved it is endemic to Sardinia. Plant seed remains have been found on the island dating back some three thousand two hundred years. So, if Cannonau wine was produced on the Island in 1197BC it would surely be one of the Mediterranean's oldest vintages. My favourite Cannonau is Nepente di Oliena from the province of Nuoro. It comes from grapes grown on a kind of soil extremely rare in Italy, a clay similar in composition to the one where the Champagne of Reims is cultivated. Nepente was also a wine celebrated by the famous early twentieth century Italian poet Gabriele D'Annunzio. The Abruzzese poet, who was only nineteen years old at that time, said of the Cannonau: *"I dedicate my body and my soul to you, island wine may you unceasingly flow to the drinking cup and from the cup to the gullet. May I rejoice at your smell till my last breath. May my nose have always your vermilion colour"*. I have to add that Gabriele D'Annunzio was also famous for having one of his own ribs removed so he could masturbate with his mouth! Oh, the joy of trivia. I finish the wine and head back home to light the fire.

I'm told that olive wood is excellent for open fires. It's extremely dense so burns very, very slowly but also gives off a wonderful smell. Nothing beats a log fire and I immediately start to feel warmer, the combination of burning wood and Cannonau really hitting the spot. I flip on the TV hoping to find a bit of light music or an old film but disappointingly tune into the Italian version of Big Brother – Grande Fratello. It appears to be much the same as the British programme - a load of stupid people stuck in a house snogging and arguing. I have to say that there is a lot more nudity in the Italian version. You do actually see breasts. I turn off the TV and go in search of a Bible and Luke 2:11.

I'm not a religious man so relish the opportunity of turning The Nativity into a really good comedy especially in a culture totally consumed by Catholicism. The cast is a manageable ten this time made up of the best actors from A Midsummer Night's Dream. The show itself only has to be half an hour long but plenty of time to get in some gags.

CHAPTER TEN

Before rehearsals start I make another attempt to get my *Permesso di Soggiorno*. I arrive at the same place at 8.45am and thankfully this time it's open.

The plastic seats are uncomfortable but I know I'm only going to have to wait fifteen minutes before the office officially opens and luckily I'm first in the queue. The door is slightly ajar and I can hear some sort of argument going on inside. From what I can understand they are complaining about a colleague for her lack of professionalism and it's getting quite heated. 9am comes and goes and they are still at it. At 9.15am the door opens and a portly woman comes out and disappears down the corridor. At last. My trousers were beginning to stick to the chair. Two minutes later she comes back carrying a tray with three cups of coffee and brioche, goes back into the room and starts complaining again – about a colleague's lack of professionalism! I can feel my anger bubbling away inside and at 9.30am decide to knock on the door. '*Aspettate fuori finché non vi chiamo*' - Wait outside we're busy is the reply. I resist the temptation to go out and find the nearest gun shop and instead start pacing up and down the corridor to try and relieve some of the tension.

Finally, after an hour's wait, I'm shown into the office. The portly woman is sitting behind a desk and I take the vacant seat in front of her. I hand over my passport and contract for the flat and after some heavy scrutiny she asks me if I have five thousand euros in the bank. What?! She tells me that I can get a *Permesso di Soggiorno* if I can prove I have five thousand euros in the bank and won't be a burden to the social system or go out begging. She further adds that without a work contract I'm not entitled to health care even if I am a European citizen. She suggests I get private medical insurance. Ridiculous.

I leave the office seething. Fortunately I do have five thousand euros in the bank in England (thanks to the sale of the flat I owned in London) but what if I didn't? 'I'm sorry Sir you can't come and live in Italy despite being a European citizen because you're not rich enough' Shameful. The system is flawed because you could always ask somebody to lend you the money long enough for it to show up on a bank statement and then give it back. As for the health care I need to get better informed but I know one thing for sure, I'm not going out to buy private medical insurance. When I get a moment I'll call the British embassy in Rome. I get into the Punto and go in search of a gun shop.

Ironically we are rehearsing in the same place as before courtesy of the Orfanotrofio Figlie Di Maria. If they only knew that the actor playing the part of Mary, Antonello Foddis, is a professional transvestite I think it would be safe to say that we would have to find somewhere else to work. Yes, it's true, Mary will be played by a male actor in drag and will arrive in Piazza Azuni in the back of a real ambulance (thanks to the city council) accompanied by 'Like a Virgin' by Madonna. That should get the crowd going but just as a precaution I prepare to leave the country anyway.

The rehearsals fly by and before I know it it's the day of the performance. We're scheduled to start at 8pm and with the stage, lights and music all set up in the square we are ready to go. There's about a hundred and fifty people in the piazza and thousands more out Christmas shopping so I'm hoping the sound of the ambulance will draw a bigger crowd. People normally get drawn to accidents or a police presence by some sort of macabre curiosity. I'm just hoping they won't be too pissed off when they find out it's a bible story. Their thirst for blood may well turn out to be a thirst for mine.

At 8.30pm, the obligatory half an hour late, the ambulance screams into action and makes its way from a side street into the Piazza. Pandemonium erupts. People start running up the main drag to see what's going on and people already in the square start pushing onlookers aside to make room for the ambulance. The deafening noise of the siren ricochets off the surrounding walls further adding to the confusion. As it comes to a stop in the centre of the square there is a deathly hush as two stony faced paramedics and two equally stony faced ambulance drivers step out of the vehicle and make their way to the back. Just as the back doors open Madonna blasts over the speakers and there, sitting on a gurney in the back of the ambulance, is Antonello 'Maria' Foddis in full drag. I have to say he looks stunning in blond curly wig, high stiletto shoes, figure hugging red dress and nine months pregnant. There is a huge cheer from the crowd as they wheel him out and onto the stage and it's at this point that I know two things. The first is that we have the crowd's attention and they will watch the rest of the show, the second is that we got away with it and I won't have to leave the country.

You can never be one hundred percent sure that certain material won't offend people and sometimes the only way to find out is to try it.

Today I'm making my last attempt to get my *Permesso di Soggiorno* and head back to my favourite place in the world – L'Ufficio Stranieri. I have a copy of my bank statement from the UK and my newly purchased Remington 44 Magnum with ivory grip. As I walk up to the first floor office I do a quick translation of 'Go ahead, make my day' which comes out as *Vai avanti, rallegrami la giornata.* Let's hope I don't have to use it.

This time there's no waiting for idle gossip. I walk straight in (Morricone music playing in my head), look Signora civil servant in the eye, and hand over the new documents. My fingers hover nervously over my new ivory handle - *Vai avanti, rallegrami la giornata.* I think I say it a bit too loudly. She looks up from the papers, narrows her eyes and goes for the rubber stamp. In what can only be described as the consummate precision of a lifetime of bureaucratic service she spins the stamp through 360 degrees before slamming it down with a well-practised authoritarian thud on my paper work. A couple of swift signatures later and I'm holding my *Permesso di Soggiorno.* She's a very lucky woman, she will never know how close she came. I coolly walk out of the room and close the door. I won't be back.

I head back to England to spend the holidays with my mum and the rest of the family. It's already bad enough that I live in a different country and I know my mother would be devastated if I didn't come home for Christmas. Unfortunately she won't fly so popping over to Sardinia for the weekend is not really an option. If she does finally come she will have to take the Eurostar to Paris, take another train from Paris to Marseilles and then the overnight boat to Porto

Torres. It's a long and costly journey compared to the two hour trip and fifty euros I generally pay on Ryanair.

For New Year I've been invited by Franco and Adele to spend the evening at a beach restaurant at Platamona. The place is doing a special menu for *Capodanno* and Licia says it should be a lot of fun. Intrigued to find out how the Sardinians spend New Year's Eve on the beach I accept the offer.

When we arrive it's not at all what I had imagined. The restaurant is a fifties building and like so many buildings along the 'Sassari Riviera' in need of some serious repair. And you can't see the beach thanks to a load of other equally decrepit holiday apartments obscuring the view. We go inside and into a vast room filled with round tables peopled with glum looking occupants. Fluorescent strip lights and those hideous polystyrene ceiling tiles are the icing on the cake of what looks like a cheap wedding. The place is absolutely characterless, my bathroom has more character than this restaurant and the lighting is better. There is only one thing for it – get pissed! We join Franco and Adele at their table and we get straight into the wine all of us sharing the same collective thought. The food is abundant but not hot, not very tasty and not cheap. Certainly nothing like the food I have grown to love and cherish on this island. You know it's all wrong when they bring out frozen prawn cocktails as a starter.

As usual a lot of the conversation revolves around what we are eating and with Franco continually telling jokes the evening is fun and informative. I didn't know for example that in Italy they tell *barzellette sui Carabinieri* - jokes about policeman. In England we often hear Irish jokes, in America they tell jokes about Polish people but here they tell jokes about the *Carabinieri*. Animated and with the gift of the gab I can see how Franco would be very good at his job. Of course Licia has to translate everything as I can't understand a bloody word he says.

By midnight everyone is drunk and we are enjoying ourselves despite the *locali*. The countdown is done by the Maitre D' followed by the obligatory kissing, cheering and singing. The tables are then cleared to one side and the dancing starts. Naively thinking I would be treated to a rare display of traditional *ballo Sardo* I get the Macarena and line dancing instead - *Balli di Gruppo!* What's extraordinary is that everyone knows how to do it from the children to the parents to the grandparents. Do we do this in Britain? It seems very un-Italian. Maybe I haven't been here long enough and they actually invented it. Sparing myself the embarrassment I resist the overwhelming desire to join in and order some Mirto.

A couple of hours later we make the short trip to Licia's parent's house to drop them off only to find out they have been burgled! On New Year's Eve of all things. Understandably Franco is livid and starts swearing profusely in Italian. The dogs were out and should have been on guard against anyone entering the house – unless they knew them...dun, dun, dunnnn! Adele does a quick check and fortunately nothing is missing, the only evidence is a broken window and some mess inside. I suggest calling the Carabinieri but Franco says *No, polizia.* He tells me he knows who did it and that they came looking for money. Apparently Franco has had a long running feud with a Sicilian family who own a *pasticceria* (pastry shop) in Sassari. Oh good. He doesn't tell me what the feud is about only that it's very real and that this is another in a long line of incidents.

I can't help thinking I'm now part of Franco's extended family and could be in line for a visit from the 'Pastry Mob' gunned down in a hail of cream filled *cannoli.* Fortunately there isn't much mafia activity here these days even though there is some evidence that suggests the mafia originated in Sardinia.

There are five main organized crime syndicates in Italy apart from Cosa Nostra - La Stidda (from Sicily), 'Ndrangheta (Calabrian Mafia), Sacra Corona Unita (Apulian Mafia) and Mala di Brenta (La Mafia del Brenta). But it is the better known Camorra or Gamurra that allegedly found its birth place in Sardinia. *Murra* is the Sardinia name given to a form of the game 'scissor, paper, stone' that is played religiously all over the island – it has its own league between villages. The game originated in China but made its way to Sardinia via Egypt, Greece (there is even an ancient Greek vase depicting Helena and Paris of Troy playing the game) and finally Rome where Roman soldiers coming to the island taught it to the locals. The story goes that the Gamurra first surfaced in the middle ages as a group of military vigilantes in the southern port of Cagliari. It was later taken to Naples in the 1500's by Sardinian mercenaries thus making it the oldest mafia in the world even pre-dating Sicily's Cosa Nostra. It is now known as Camorra or the Neapolitan Mafia.

Anonima Sarda or Anonima Sequestri is the name given to a certain group of people allegedly responsible for a lot of the criminal activity on the island including murder, theft and above all kidnapping (they were responsible for the kidnapping of Fabrizio De André in 1979). It is not considered to be Mafia or Camorra as it has none of the same organisational traits or hierarchy and is totally disassociated from politics. Instead it lives by a code of honour shared with the bandit population and some of the general population of central Sardinia (Nuoro, Ogliastra, Oristano and even parts of the province of Sassari). It is called the Codice Barbaricino.

Eleonora di Arborea was the *giudicessa* or judge of Arborea from 1383 to her death in 1404. She was by far the most powerful of the four *giudici* on the island and is best known for creating a set of laws which the islanders subscribed to called *Carta de Logu*. The laws were based on local customs and traditions which treated everyone as an equal. The *Carta de Logu* remained in place until the unification of Italy in 1861 when a new set of laws were introduced by Carlo Felice, the then king of Sardinia. Many of these laws were contrary to what the majority of central islanders believed to be fair – i.e. the right to be free, the right to own property etc. and by the end of the 19th century had compiled their own set of unwritten moral and social laws based on those of Eleonora di Arborea called the Codice Barbaricino which are still in existence today.

Also known as *Codice d'onore* or *Codice Vendetta* it is founded on the basic belief that all people are equal in the eyes of the natural law of the land. Under the *Codice Barbaricino* one of the worst crimes you could possibly commit is stealing livestock (in most cases sheep). By doing so you rob a person of their dignity as they can no longer provide for their family. The dignity therefore, has far more importance than the object of the crime. The penalty for such a crime under the code would be to have a fish hook placed in your tongue and pulled out by rope. Even if you were only in possession of the stolen animal you would suffer the same fate. If you killed a man in cold blood the penalty would be death by beheading but if you killed a man for revenge or as part of a vendetta you could walk away without penalty.

Orgosolo, (dubbed the bandit capital of the island due to various vendettas and feuding) averaged a murder every two months between 1901 and 1953. The town only has a population of four thousand.

On a lighter note, apart from bandits, the region is also famous for its cooking, especially one of my personal favourites - *Culurgiones.*

We say good night to Franco and Adele wishing them a Happy New Year, which under the circumstances sounds a bit forced and drive back to Sassari.

Satisfied the door is securely locked I check the bed for horse's heads and go to sleep.

Culurgiones

Serves 4

Ingredients

For the pastry

- *250g flour*
- *250g durham wheat flour*
- *1 egg*
- *pinch of salt*
- *200ml warm water*

For the filling

- *250g boiled potatoes (mashed)*
- *300g pecorino*
- *1 egg yolk*
- *14 wild mint leaves (finely chopped)*
- *pinch of salt*

Preparation

Put the flour in a mixing bowl and shape into a cone. Make a hole in the top and add the warm water, pinch of salt and the egg.

Knead until the dough becomes homogeneous and smooth (the more you knead the better it is).

In a separate bowl prepare the mixture for the filling. Add the grated cheese, the boiled mashed potatoes, the oil (gradually), the egg yolk and the chopped mint. Mix until it becomes soft.

Roll the dough until approximately 5mm thick and then cut into 6-7cm diameter discs. On one half of each disc add the filling (about the size of a walnut), then gently cover each half with the other and close applying gentle pressure.

Cook in plenty of salted boiling water and drain one by one with a perforated spoon as they come to surface.

Serve with fresh tomato sauce and plenty of grated pecorino.

Culurgiones are traditionally sewn to resemble ears of corn bringing good fortune and prosperity.

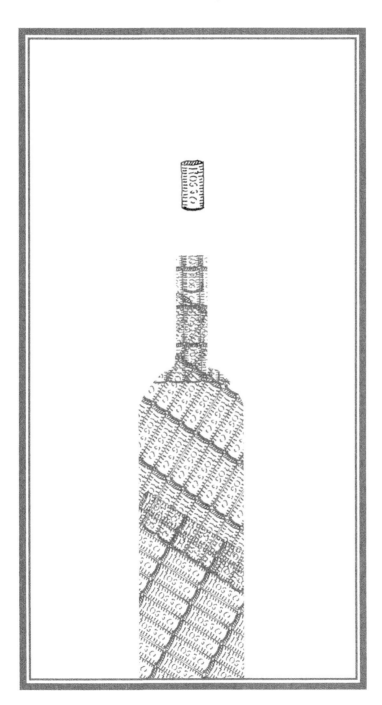

CHAPTER ELEVEN

It's February and six months have passed since I first arrived on the island. I've just returned from another trip to the UK, this time to Newcastle to do a production of the Scottish play that I adapted called 'Macbeth, Kill Bill Shakespeare'. I'm still not getting quite enough work, or work that's paid well enough, to stop me nipping back to England to earn money. I suppose it's still early days but I have realized that Sardinia is not the theatre capital of the world. Apart from the work everything is going well. If I have to travel now and again so be it, I live in a beautiful place and would not give it up for anything.

Romeo e Giulietta comes and goes at Teatro Verdi and keeps me busy up until Easter. With pretty much the same cast as A Midsummer Night's Dream the show is good and well received.

Castelsardo is about forty minutes drive north east of Sassari. Licia and I set off early in the morning taking the coast road via Platamona and onto the former Genoan stronghold previously called Castelgenovese. It's an impressive medieval town perched proudly on an outcrop of rock with spectacular views of the sea – a perfect getaway from the city grime and negative thoughts.

Going east from Platamona the *pineta* (pine wood) lined road follows the sea all the way to Castelsardo with a large choice of beaches along the route. We pass through the Marina di Sorso that serves the sun worshipers from the town of Sorso and its neighbour Sennori. The two towns are practically joined at the hip with only a couple of hundred yards of asphalt separating these old rivals (each town blames the other's men for stealing their respective women but I'm told that this is quite common between neighbouring Sardinian villages).

Legend has it that the people from Sorso stole the Fontana di Rosello from Sassari which then had to be rebuilt. It is now widely recognised that people from *Sorso* who drink from the newly named Fontana della Billellera are completely crazy as the water is cursed. The fact that the fountain is condemned makes the inhabitants as mad as a bag of chips. We don't stop.

What I notice immediately as we approach Castelsardo is the new town crouching hungrily at the feet of its historical master looking positively ugly in comparison. An impressive display of tourist tat lines the streets as we drive through this modern brightly painted centre and head up towards the castle. At the point where the new town finishes and the old town starts there is a sort of no man's land, void of any buildings as if an imaginary line had been drawn against the encroaching modernity. *Basta* the castle bellows – enough!

The road continues to spiral steeply upward until we eventually come to the historic centre. It immediately becomes obvious that unless I can get the car onto the two left wheels with the help of a small ramp we are not going any further. From what I can see the streets are so narrow it's hard to imagine even a horse and cart negotiating these tiny passageways. Maybe a Shetland pony pulling a wheelbarrow but certainly nothing bigger. We park the car on the extremely steep hill, making sure we leave it in first gear and walk the last couple of hundred meters.

Castelsardo is famous for its *artigianato,* or handcrafts, in particular *l'intreccio* or basketwork, which has expanded in the last few years due to the influx of tourists. I wouldn't say it's a multi-million dollar cottage industry but it certainly brings a lot of much needed revenue to the area all year round. Wicker, raffia, straw, reeds, asphodel leaves and dwarf palm (which is the material of choice grown locally and picked by hand) are all used to create a large variety of containers in all shapes and sizes. It's basket heaven! Bucket loads of baskets! Baskets everywhere! Bursting with baskets! Baskets! Baskets! Baskets! The castle even boasts a basket museum! I'm not a 'wicker man' myself but if it's baskets you like you have certainly come to the right place. Many of them are beautiful and we trot off to one of the many shops for a bit of basket browsing. They are not cheap but they have been made by hand and must take a long time to weave. There is even luggage made from straw – 'basket cases'. I spot a particularly nice clothes basket but at a hundred euros I think it's a bit of an expensive luxury just for my dirty shreddies. Licia buys a small bread basket at a respectable ten euros.

The old town is incredibly quiet due to the lack of vehicles and a beautiful place to get lost in and to explore the tiny little cobbled alleyways. Every so often we come across a little old lady dressed in black sitting in a doorway weaving peacefully away with a pile of date palms beside her. Plants and flowers adorn nearly every building adding to the tranquillity and signalling the start of spring. The views are some of the best I've seen and I'm told that on a perfectly clear day you can see Corsica eleven kilometres away across the Bocche di Bonifacio.

Castelsardo used to be a commercial port but now plays host only to tourist traffic so it seems fitting that we stop at 'The Bounty' restaurant for a seafood lunch (did Captain

Bligh and young Fletcher Christian stop off in Castelsardo for a bit of pre mutiny tucker before heading off to Tahiti?).

If you take away the maritime window dressing (anchors, fish nets, oars etc.) the restaurant is a beautiful old vaulted cellar, the ceiling a typical feature of the island's architecture. Unfortunately it doesn't have a view whereas the restaurant up the hill does but is twice the price.

One of the town's specialities is lobster. They say that *l'aragosta* in north west Sardinia are some of the best in the world due to the clear blue water that they live and feed in. The lobster from this particular region (between Bosa and Castelsardo) is so good that they are planning to classify it in much the same way as they do with wine and cheese giving it a DOP (*Denominazione di Origine Protetta*) certification - a mark of origin and quality. Restaurants all around the north west compete once a year to see who can cook the best lobster dish. Out of the twelve restaurants that participated last year here are the three dishes that came in first, second and third - In first place was *Ravioli all'aragosta con crema di finocchio, salsa di bufala e zafferano e pane al datterino* (lobster ravioli with cream of fennel, buffalo mozzarella sauce, saffron and handmade tomato bread). In second place *Morbido cuore della regina del mare con croccante di fiori di zucca* (soft heart of the queen of the sea with crispy courgette flowers) and in third place *Suppa kin aligusta* or *Zuppa di aragosta alla castellanese con crostini di pane casareccio* (Castelsardo lobster soup with toasted casareccio bread).

Wanting to try the local dish we order *Suppa kin aligusta* as it's called in dialect. If you want to cook it at home preparation is not for the faint hearted.

Zuppa di Aragosta alla Castellanese con Crostini di Pane Casareccio

Serves 4
Ingredients
- *600g of live lobster*
- *half a finely chopped onion*
- *200g of mature chopped tomatoes*
- *litre of water*
- *1 cup of Vermentino (or similar dry, crisp white wine)*
- *1/2 teaspoon chili powder*
- *chopped basil and parsley to season*
- *1 clove garlic finely chopped*
- *1 cup of cognac or brandy*
- *salt*

Preparation

Clean the lobster thoroughly and then chop it while still alive. Chop the tail into medallions, split the head in two and the body into quarters. Remove any tomalley (the green liver of a lobster) and any roe and set aside. Put the chopped shell pieces of the lobster in a litre of hot water and put aside for later.

Sauté the onion, garlic, pepper and chilli in extra virgin olive oil then add the tomalley, roe and white wine and cook for a few minutes. Add the tomatoes and lightly brown. At this point, add the rest of the lobster (saving the water for later) and fry everything for five minutes. Pour on the brandy or cognac and flambé.

Now start adding the water a bit at a time. Add salt, season with basil and parsley and cook for 15-20 minutes. Place the lobster in a serving dish, reduce the broth for a few minutes and then serve with croutons of crusty bread.

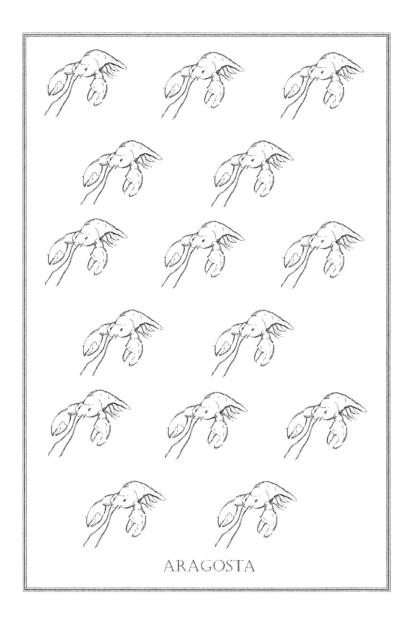

ARAGOSTA

Try as I might I'm finding it very difficult to have a bad meal in Sardinia. With the exception of New Year's Eve and the messing about I've been doing in my kitchen everything has been of the highest quality. I could live here - Oh, I do.

We work off lunch with another stroll around the basket capital of the world and pop into the Church of Santa Maria famed locally for its sacred *Cristu Nieddu* or Black Christ. It's a fourteenth century crucifix with a black Jesus nailed to it. I bet if we go into the new town we can find a plastic souvenir replica complete with afro - or even worse, a woven one. The medieval church is also the focal point for the procession of *Lunissanti* which takes place the Monday before Easter. It's a pre-dawn torch lit affair carried out by members of The Brotherhood of Holy Cross Oratory, complete with Gregorian singing and black cloaks it's a bit spooky.

At 4pm we decide to make a move back to Sassari. Luckily the Punto is still there and hasn't rolled back down the hill into the new town destroying some of those lovely concrete buildings. We drive through the ghetto of the future, resisting the temptation to stop and look for a plastic *Cristu Nieddu* and join the road back to Platamona.

I have a good memory of Castelsardo (the old town that is) and make a point to come back soon.

BASILICO

CHAPTER TWELVE

The summer brings an onslaught of visitors from Britain. One thing you must be prepared for if you live in a hot country is all your friends and family coming over looking for a cheap holiday. What you don't realise is that you will end up spending just as much money as they do. Driving to the beach every day, *aperitivi* in the piazza every evening, restaurants every night soon mounts up to holiday spending and when you have a constant stream of visitors it's a fuck of a lot of money.

Because my apartment is small and open plan most people have to stay on the sofa downstairs but for the less familiar guests and couples I have to book a hotel or B&B.

I'd been given the number of a bed and breakfast called *Casachiara* (clear house) by one of the theatre crowd and decide to go and check it out. It would be useful to know who runs it and whether it's any good or not (I have stayed in some terrible places that make the prison in Midnight Express look like Raffles).

The location is perfect, it's just off Piazza Azuni in *il centro storico* on Vicolo Bertolinis. I arrive at an enormous *palazzo* and press the buzzer above the leather embossed sign - Casachiara. I climb the staircase (it must be at least ten feet wide and covered with original tiles) and eventually arrive at the *secondo piano*.

Standing at the door of the bed and breakfast is a young man, no older than twenty-six or twenty-seven, with long, long dread locks and arms covered with tattoos. Holding a pair of drumsticks he introduces himself as Luigi. Now if you were the sort of person who judged people by their appearances you would probably leave immediately for the nearest hotel. The tattoos are well drawn and not blurred like prison tattoos which is a good sign. I strain to see if Sardinians write 'I love mum' in Italian – *Ti amo mamma* but I don't want my blatant curiosity to be that obvious.

The apartment is beautiful with many of its original features including tiles, doors and ceilings. The terracotta coloured breakfast room has a huge, long wooden table with a good assortment of Sardinian books lining the walls. The place has a warm, cosy feel and it's obvious that Luigi wants people to feel like they're at home. He shows me the *cucina* which is uncharacteristically eclectic compared to the rest of the apartment - Laurie Lee meets Italy. The bedrooms are minimally furnished with tasteful decor, air conditioning and TV. At thirty euros a night including breakfast it's a bargain. Luigi turns out to be a really nice guy and we chat easily about Sassari, Sardinia and Music. He tells me that as well as running a B&B he is also a *batterista* or drummer in a local band but quickly adds that he only practices when guests are out. I definitely wouldn't have put the two occupations together, it does seem like a bit of a contradiction in terms – if you want a quiet bed for the night go and stay with a drummer.

Well, it looks like I've found a good place for people to stay. It's cheap, clean and close, and as long as Luigi keeps his drumming to a minimum - quiet.

I've done my secret pre-tanning on the terrace and I'm ready to hit the beaches. Having lots of people over does give me the excuse to explore some of the surrounding coast and with only factor five in hand I'm good to go. My good friend and colleague Bruce French has arrived and I'm excited about giving him the grand tour of the island and showing off my new life in the Med. Bruce is a freelance designer who as well as designing for theatre and opera also works with big music artists such as The Rolling Stones, Björk and Pulp. We have worked together for about eight years and the older Bruce gets the more he looks like Ronnie Woods. He's a seasoned traveller and I'm curious to know what he thinks of Sardinia. Having spent the night on my sofa I can tell he's looking forward to a deep sleep on soft white sand. I can't say I blame him. My sofa is only five feet long and he's six feet tall. What more does he want - it's free isn't it?

We jump into the Punto and head for a beach called Le Bombarde. It's about three kilometres north of Mussolini's dream town of Fertilia and takes us forty minutes from Sassari. I'd been told that Le Bombarde is a beach for *ragazzi* or young people but I hardly think that Bruce and I, being in our thirties, qualify as being old. How young can these people be?

I twice miss the turning for the somewhat discreetly marked road that takes us down to the parking area and can't help thinking that the locals have hidden it on purpose just to keep the tourists out. We park the car in the fifty cents an hour car park and head down to the *spiaggia*. It's a beautiful white sandy bay with crystal clear water, *pineta* and wonderful views of Alghero to the south and Capo Caccia to the north. Bruce is impressed. Is it the view or the beautiful young girls? It's towel to towel *ragazzi* and nobody looks older than twenty.

We spot a small opening in the sand and with stomachs sucked in tightly make our way down and into the lazy waxed mass of brown semi-nakedness. As coolly as possible we lay out our towels and finally breathe out. This is not a beach this is a beauty pageant, a catwalk, a fashion show, a Miss World and Mr Universe competition all rolled into one. How is it that Sardinians are such perfect human specimens? Maybe because there is such a high life expectancy on the island they are born with longer lasting super human bodies? Bruce spends most of the afternoon looking remarkably like a Meerkat.

The next day we try another beach called La Stalla that we'd been told by Licia is much more our sort of *spiaggia* - for old people then. I'm sure when we left Le Bombarde yesterday somebody said '*Arrivederci nonni*' - 'Goodbye granddads'. Cheeky whippersnappers.

La Stalla is another four kilometres beyond Le Bombarde at a place called Porto Conte on the road to Capo Caccia. The beach is spectacular. It's a long *pineta* lined curve of beautiful white sand completely uncompromised by buildings and with hardly anyone on it a veritable paradise. Plus the parking is free.

We spend an extremely lazy day swimming, chatting, sipping cold Ichnusa (from one of the various beach shacks selling *panini e bevande*) and generally doing nothing.

Bruce tells me he's starting to feel depressed living in London and is considering moving abroad. He's fed up with the weather, the prices and the trains. Sardinia, he says, is a prime candidate for relocation. Obviously being a freelance designer it's much easier for him to work from anywhere in the world and send stuff back via the internet. It's not as if he's tied down to a 9 to 5 job and he could always jump on a plane if it was absolutely necessary – a bit like I do. 'Who dares wins' I tell him but can't help thinking that it's a vacational hazard (if there is such a thing) to be on holiday and dream of moving. His motives become a little clearer as we watch an Ursula Andress look alike (complete with seventies white bikini) emerge from the sea holding a conch in a scene reminiscent of Dr No. OK, she doesn't have a conch but the rest is true.

After a satisfying five hours on the beach we decide to head to Alghero via Capo Caccia to the north for a quick look at the famous headland. Capo Caccia is an enormous wedge of limestone rock dominating the sky line with its impressive cliffs and spectacular views. It's a national park and nature reserve covering almost three thousand hectors of land and at three hundred meters at its highest point a popular place for suicides. It's the Beachy Head of the Med.

As well as its wildlife it is particularly famous for its labyrinth of caves discovered in 1700 the longest of which is the imaginatively named Grotte di Nettuno, or Neptune's Grotto that stretches for some two and a half kilometres underground.

You can get to the caves by boat from Alghero which costs about ten euros but what they don't tell you until you are on the boat is that it costs another ten euros to get into the caves. If you don't have the extra ten euros you have to sit on the boat and wait until the excursion has finished. It's not as if they have a *bancomat*, or cash point inside the grotto, that would give a whole new meaning to 'a hole in the wall' but they don't even take cards – *Bastardi*!

The cheaper option is to take the 656 steps down the Escala del Cabirol (goat's steps) from the top of the cliff but remember you have to walk the 656 steps back up. Bruce and I decide to do it another day and opt for a cold beer at the Capo Caccia Café.

The sunset is a must here and we catch an hour of the incredible *tramonto* before driving to Alghero for dinner.

Once called Barcelloneta, or Little Barcelona because of its Spanish invasion in 1353, Alghero is a beautiful historic fishing port boasting an impressive array of Catalan/Gothic style architecture. Following an uprising the Spanish garrison based in Alghero was butchered making way for an influx of Catalan settlers who stamped their mark firmly on the town. The Algherese were banished from the town and laws were passed limiting the number of native Sards who could enter in a sort of 'ethnic cleansing' operation. Subsequently Catalano or Algherese is still spoken by some people to this day. The town is a mix between a fishing port and a tourist resort and by no means reliant on the latter for economic stability. The sprawling new town is testament to the relatively new and flourishing tourist industry stretching for miles along the coast comprising mostly of 1960's hotels and apartment complexes.

It's the height of summer and the old town is heaving with lobster coloured English and Germans (easily spottable amongst the evenly tanned, well dressed Italians). We wander the packed puzzle of streets before settling for an aperitif on the old *bastioni* with its amazing views of Capo Caccia and the last of the *tramonto*. It's not the cheapest place for an aperitif but certainly the most spectacular. Being Saturday night finding a restaurant that isn't fully booked is proving a little difficult. We finally settle for a beautifully vaulted affair called Al Vecchio Mulino (To the Old Mill) on Via Roma. We both order one of the *Specialità della Città – Tonno all'Algherese*.

Tonno all'Algherese

Serves 4

Ingredients

- *1.2 kg fresh tuna steaks*
- *1 cup of white wine*
- *30g pitted black olives*
- *3 bay leaves*
- *1/2 stick of celery (chopped)*
- *1 medium onion (chopped)*
- *1 cup of extra virgin olive oil*
- *juice of one lemon*
- *1 cup of water*
- *salt*

Preparation

Marinate the tuna in a bowl with the water and lemon juice for two hours. Put the olive oil in a pan and gently fry the onion, celery and bay leaves. Add the tuna and cook over a low heat for about 10 minutes, turning occasionally to cook evenly. Pour in the white wine and add the pitted black olives. Season with salt and cook covering the pan with a lid for a few minutes. Done.

Both of us are flagging and decide to call it a night and head back to Sassari. It's always amazing how a day in the sun followed by a couple of beers can really take it out of you. I'm utterly exhausted and still have to drive the forty minutes home. I hope we don't get pulled over by the Carabinieri. Berlusconi brought in a new law whereby if you are caught over the limit they can confiscate your car, sell it at auction and keep the profits. How's that for a deterrent?

We'll come back and explore Alghero another day.

CIOGGHITTA

Today is *Ciogghitta* day so if it's eating snails that you like then no place is better than Rinnovata Taverna Bellieni in Sassari. Every August teams of two people compete against each other to see how many snails they can consume in the shortest time. *Succiadura di ciogga minudda* or sucking the small snails as it's known in Sassaresse is an art form and nobody seems to be better "suckers" of the intrepid snails than Antonio Capeccia and Antonio Pintus from team "Arcade Las Vegas" winners for the second consecutive year. These two young men consumed a record 115 snails in just two minutes. It's not just a matter of speed, but technique - head down, right hand full of snails, left goes to the mouth and so on. Cheered on by a huge crowd of people who have invaded Via Bellieni they empty the first bowl and fill the second as they work in well-practiced tandem to win the coveted 'Ciogghitta d'Oro' - The Golden Snail. Strong competition comes from team *'Ti si magnani li can*i' who take the silver snail closely followed by the aggressive "*Cioggana di Dozzi*', who take the bronze. In fourth place are the '*Caracoles*' who win a dinner at the restaurant '*La Guardiola*' in Castelsardo. The fifth ranked team get a ten-pound bag of '*ciogga minudda'*. This is a unique, fun event that I would recommend to anyone passing through this part of the island in August.

The jewel in the crown of the north west's beaches must be La Pelosa at Stintino. Fine white sand lapped by clear, shallow, turquoise water gives one the impression of being in the Caribbean rather than the Med. It makes Platamona look like land fill and that's saying something as Platamona isn't a bad beach at all. Directly in front of us is the tiny Isola Piana and beyond this the home of the small white donkeys - Asinara.

It's Sunday and the beach is absolutely mobbed - another towel fest. We manage to squeeze in next to a modest Italian family of about twenty who have decided to make a small village in the middle of the *spiaggia*. They have everything from flippers and inflatable boats to tables and a whole gang of freezer boxes. They even have a small gazebo. The mother, and obviously head of the family, must be near on sixteen stone (excluding the gold jewellery) and sits wedged into one of those very small beach chairs chatting loudly to her chubby young son, Tonino. The rest of the large *famiglia*, as if competing for weight supremacy, lie beached on various towels and sun loungers greedily snacking away. *Ciao!* the Italian equivalent of 'Hello' magazine seems to be the reading material of choice amongst the women and *Lo Sport* amongst the men. They are in this for the long haul.

On our one square meter of sand Bruce and I sit like the polite Englishmen we are and watch events unfold in this enthralling beach-com. After an hour or so of relative tranquillity there's a sudden commotion in the neighbouring village. Activity of any sort can only mean one thing - feeding time. I kid you not, within the space of a few minutes, as if from nowhere, the gazebo is transformed into a temporary dining room. Complete with table, chairs, tablecloth, plates, glasses, cutlery, napkins, water and wine it is an extraordinary achievement. Everybody else on the beach seems to think it's the most natural thing in the world so why do I feel like I'm lying on the floor of a restaurant.

Now for the food. I give Bruce a running commentary just in case there are some dishes he doesn't recognise.

So, they start off with the basics – olives, cheese and sausage, just as a light appetizer. Then we are into the main courses. First out of the freezer box is ravioli with some sort of *ragù* sauce followed close behind by another one of my personal favourites *melazane alla parmigiana (baked aubergines)*. Next up is rice salad, a common hot weather dish in Italy usually made with eggs, cheese, mayonnaise and vegetables preserved in vinegar. I'm getting hungry just watching them - even one of the dishes would suffice. A whole stack of *fettine impanate* appear (veal fried in breadcrumbs) and are passed around with *spianata* (a type of flat bread a bit like Indian nahn). The *fettine impanate* are wrapped in the *spianata* and eaten a bit like a *panino* – with mayonnaise. The sweating has started but they forge ahead unmoved in the searing heat, still managing to *chiacchierare* (chat) with their mouths *piene di cibo*. It's at this point that tubby Tonino disappears only to return ten minutes later with a tray full of chips! Do these people have no shame?

Melenzane fritte (fried aubergine) and the marvellous *zucchine ripiene* (stuffed courgettes) complete the savoury courses and I can only imagine what they are going to have for dessert.

Bruce says he's a bit peckish and I have to agree. We order a couple of *tramezzini* at the beach shack (we don't want to overdo it) and head quickly back to the towels not wanting to miss a minute of beach-com action. They're still eating. No surprises there. It's melon, ice-cream and coffee at what looks like the end of feeding time. Now they are going to do one of two things - either sleep or mate and I really hope it's not the latter.

ZUCCHINE RIPIENE

Zucchine Ripiene

Serves 4

Ingredients

- *6-7 medium-sized courgettes*
- *half an onion*
- *olive oil*
- *salt*
- *1 egg*
- *handful of bread crumbs*
- *grated parmesan (from 50 to 150 g according to taste)*
- *250g of minced beef*

Wash the courgettes and cut lengthways into two halves. Using a teaspoon gently scoop out the soft pulp from the centre and set aside. Fry the onion with a little olive oil until slightly golden. Add the soft pulp together with the minced meat and gently cook. Add salt to taste. When cooked let the mixture cool for approximately 10 minutes. Add the grated cheese and the egg and mix well.

Put the courgette shells in boiling water for two minutes. Take them out and remove the excess water by patting down with a kitchen towel. Fill the shells with the pre-prepared mixture, cover lightly with breadcrumbs and cook in the oven for about twenty minutes at 180 degrees.

Zucchine Ripiene, Dolce

Serves 4

Ingredients

- 6-7 medium-sized courgettes
- half an onion
- olive oil
- 1 egg
- 1/2 cup of warm milk
- 100g dried bread
- tablespoon of sugar (optional)

Prepare the courgettes as above. Add the soft pulp to the pan and gently cook. When cooked let it cool for approximately 10 minutes. Add the egg and the bread previously soaked in a little warm milk. Add the tablespoon of sugar and mix together.

Place the courgette shells in boiling water for two minutes. Take them out and remove the excess water by patting down with kitchen towel. Fill the shells with the pre-prepared *mixture and cook in the oven for approximately twenty minutes at 180 degrees.*

Vegetarian version
Same as above but the minced meat should be replaced by sweetcorn (2 tablespoons or more according to taste) and 2 finely chopped carrots. Cook together with the courgette pulp.
Instead of grated parmesan add finely chopped "Dolce Sardo" (or gruyere).

***

Despite the snoring neighbours the rest of the day is relaxing. La Pelosa is a truly remarkable place and certainly the best looking beach I've been to so far. Next time I come I'll make sure it's not a Sunday. As far as a quiet paradise is concerned La Stalla is the *spiaggia* for me. Bruce is *d'accordo*.

Driving around to the various beaches over the past few days I've become aware of something that I've been trying to ignore – *immondizia*. It's not so much on the beaches but more on the way to them that there is a distinct amount of rubbish. Like a light dandruff it peppers the road side and congregates in lay-bys totally without challenge. You would have thought that a place so dependent on tourism would care more about the natural environment but it appears not to be the case and is almost ignored by the different local *commune* or councils that make up the north west of the island. I'm not saying it's horrendous but it is noticeable. Even at Capo Caccia, a national park for goodness sake, I couldn't believe the amount of litter adorning the Sardinian gorse like synthetic snow. Again you would think that the people who owned the café would take some responsibility and make sure the rubbish didn't accumulate even if the council won't. It's a false economy in a place that can ill afford economic misadventure.

Tourism represents the main industry on the island with 2,721 active tourist related companies and 189,239 rooms across hotels, B&B's etc. In 2008 there were 2,363,496 arrivals (up 1.4% on 2007). In the same year, the airports on the island registered 11,896,674 passengers (up 1.24% on 2007). So you would think that the authorities would protect their investment and keep the island clean. Despite these figures unemployment remains the highest in Italy fluctuating between 18% and 21% where the national average is 9.5%. Even more of a reason for sustainable growth in the tourist sector. La Nuova Sardegna pointed out that with the exception of two other regions (Campania and Calabria) to find worse figures you would have to go to Bulgaria where the unemployment rate in one region is a staggering 75%.

I stop the Punto and make Bruce get out of the car with a plastic bag and start picking up litter.

CHAPTER THIRTEEN

The stream of visitors continues throughout the summer months and with every new arrival I add another layer of tan. I don't remember a time when I was more *abbronzato*.

Casachiara turns out to be a success story with nobody complaining about midnight drumming but complimenting Luigi on his particularly good breakfasts. His combination of sweet and sour is a winner. *Prosciutto, formaggio e pane* for the more savoury palette and brioche or a large choice of Sardinian pastries for the sweeter toothed traveller.

Work in the summer months is slow. All the theatres shut down from June to September in Sassari as nobody wants to spend time indoors. Even though the main theatres have air conditioning, psychologically people associate being inside with being hot which is not necessarily the case. I have to say that spending the month of *Luglio* stuck inside a dark theatre isn't that appealing especially when you know that everybody's on the beach enjoying themselves. It would be different in the UK. With rain throughout the summer being inside would be the logical place of choice. It's no coincidence that they have the Edinburgh Theatre Festival in August you know.

My final guests for the *l'estate* are another friend and colleague Simon Woods and his wife Den. Simon was chief executive of Birmingham School of Speech and Drama but with itchy feet is looking to make a new career for himself as a film producer. As the manager that brought UB40 to fame in the eighties he is not short of a bit of vision and film producing is certainly not out of his league.

After a week, while having lunch in Bar Barroccu on the *Corso,* Simon hands me a script that Den found for a play called *La Mandragola* (The Mandrake Root), a little known farce written by Machiavelli in the early sixteenth century. Machiavelli wrote a farce? Simon is setting up a production company called 'European Drama Network' with the purpose of making new movies of classic plays, the first of which will be *La Mandragola.* The play is set in Florence but Simon wants to film it in Sassari as it would be cheaper and asks me if I would like to direct it and write the screenplay. After a quick read I jump at the chance. I've never directed a full length feature film and relish the opportunity.

Of course it's not that simple. Simon has yet to raise the *denaro* to make it so it's not as if we are going to start filming next week. Well, it's always good to have irons in the fire and I trust Simon's ability to find the cash. One thing I know about Mr Woods is that when he commits to something he will see it through no matter what. The film will happen but he thinks it's at least a year away.

Having made short work of a plate of *tramezzini* we order the fabulous king of Sardinian desserts – *Seadas*. After a little cajoling, the couple who run the bar, Angelo and Donatella, agree to give me the family recipe as cooked by Donatella's grandmother and passed on to her daughter Nonna Rosina.

Seadas

Serves 8

Ingredients

- *1kg flour*
- *250g "strutto" (creamy pork fat at room temperature)*
- *100g sugar*
- *2 eggs*
- *zest of 1 lemon*
- *honey*
- *zest of 1 orange*

For the filling

- *1kg of fresh pecorino cheese*
- *juice and zest of 1 lemon*
- *250g sugar*

Preparation

Sift the flour into a bowl, make a hole in the middle and add a pinch of salt. Add the egg, diced "strutto" (you can use butter if you prefer) and lemon zest. Knead for at least 10 minutes until you get a smooth, firm dough. Set aside to rest for 20 minutes.

Coarsely grate the cheese and mix with the lemon juice and zest.

Roll out the dough into a 2.5mm thick sheet and cut circles of 8cm in diameter. Place a spoon of the mixture in the middle of a circle, brush the edges with egg and cover with another circle, pressing the edges firmly together.

Fry the Seadas in a good amount of olive oil and then drain on kitchen paper. Heat the honey with the orange zest until it's nice and runny, pour onto the Seadas and enjoy.

***

It's been a year since my first conversation with Simon and we are no further forward with the film. I know it takes time to find the capital and I'm in no great hurry, as soon as he is ready he'll let me know.

The last year has been *su e giù*, up and down. My relationship with Licia finished a couple of months ago, both of us mutually agreeing that it had come to a natural end. It was good while it lasted as they say. I had somebody special to share my Sardinian experience with, somebody to talk to and now that I'm single I feel very much on my own again. We are still very good friends which is a good thing as I can still get antiques at a discount! But seriously, in a small town where you never know who you are going to run into it's better to still be friends rather than enemies. Antiques and small town apart, Licia is a wonderful person and I have no regrets about the time we spent together.... I'll miss those dogs.

I've done six shows over the past year - three of them in Sassari, one in England and two in Germany. In fact one of the shows in Germany was a remount of 'The Merchant of Venice' that I had done over here earlier in the year (different company but pretty much the same actors). I had been asked by the Neuss Shakespeare Festival to produce and direct 'Macbeth Kill Bill Shakespeare' for their summer programme but they also expressed an interest in the Italian shows I had been directing. So, I ended up going to Germany with The Merchant of Venice in Italian and Macbeth in English.

In order to do both shows at the same time I had a cast of British actors together with British technicians come over to Sardinia to rehearse simultaneously with the Italian cast. What was great about the experience was that the Sardinians had the opportunity of working with and observing highly experienced practitioners from abroad. It was also wonderful to see a home grown Sardinian production taken out of the island to a prestigious festival in Germany.

Il Mercante di Venezia had great success in Sassari and despite being in Italian was equally successful in Neuss. I think a lot of its international appeal was again down to its visual content.

In the original version at Teatro Verdi the character of Bassanio had a live piglet on stage as a provocation to Shylock. When I first suggested the idea to the producer of a *maiale vivo* on stage he didn't bat an eyelid and the very next day we were off to a Sardinian pig farm to audition pigs. The owner of the pig farm (a friend of a friend of a friend of the producer), expecting our arrival, had all his *maiale* on parade and was obviously very proud of the fact that one of his pigs was going to be a big star. Getting it back to Sassari in the boot of the producer's fiat panda was definitely the highlight of the day. The biggest problem was that we had to keep it for a week in the bathroom at the place where we were rehearsing. Every time we were in the middle of a scene you could hear a grunting, a rooting, or a squealing making it almost impossible to concentrate. Now don't get me wrong it was a very big bathroom with plenty of space, air and water. Certainly five star accommodation compared to what it was used to. We bought a lead and every day we would take Romeo (we couldn't think of a better name) for a walk to get it used to being around people and noise. I could almost hear the people in Sassari saying '*Guarda, eccolo l'Inglese pazzo!*' – look, there goes the mad Englishman! They were probably right.

The sixteen piece brass band that I needed proved even easier to get than the pig even though they only had to come on and play for five minutes (*Banda Musicale* are ten a penny in Sassari and as they are often playing outside my window at eight in the morning, very easy to find).

If you want to have a live animal on stage in Britain there are so many rules and regulations it's almost an impossible thing to achieve but in Italy, *non c'è problema*. The same with a brass band. It would probably have cost me a fortune in the UK but in Italy they did it for free.

Of course the Germans wanted the show complete with pig and band so when we arrived they had both waiting for us. The German band had already learnt the same tune as the Italian band and was no problem but the pig was a nightmare. It just wouldn't go on stage for love nor truffles. The more we tried the more it squealed as if we were strangling it. The German producer, Reiner Weiss, called in a vet who suggested we tranquilise the poor animal but at that point I decided to cut it rather than have Bassanio drag its sedated, limp body across the stage. It just goes to show that you should always do your own casting or suffer the consequences.

The next show in Sassari was a version of The Genesis, again Tommaso finding the money to do a bible story in the open air. Once more I couldn't pass up the opportunity to turn it into a comedy and had God dressed as a pimp arrive in a Limousine in Piazza Italia (Sassari's main square) accompanied by a *prostituta*. If you want to rent a Limo for the morning in Sassari there is only one company that can supply a car like that and it's very *costoso*. For a two hour hire we ended up paying three hundred euros. I originally wanted God to arrive in a helicopter but was told it would be too expensive.

The third show in Sassari was a real disaster. The same company that produced The Merchant of Venice had been asked to do *La Bisbetica Domata* (The Taming of The Shrew) as part of *Sassari Estate* (the outdoor summer festival that happens every year organised by the council). I had directed the show as an outdoor production to be staged in a makeshift open air theatre next to the Chiesa di Santa Maria on the edge of the old town. The day before technical rehearsals were due to start I went down to check out *il teatro*. To my horror almost half the auditorium was under water. We decided at the last moment to move the show to Teatro Verdi which just happened to be free. Of course the show was a shambles because it wasn't designed to go into Teatro Verdi but for an outdoor platform stage. A theatre the size of Teatro Verdi needs a lot of lights, different scenery and different movements for the actors. I did my best.

I'm still in my little *Mansarda* in Via Largo Infermeria San Pietro and very much enjoying my summer *terrazzo* and winter *camino*. I seem to have accumulated a lot of stuff since I've been in Italy (mostly antique furniture) and might have to think about finding a bigger place in the not too distant future. At least somewhere big enough to swing a *gatto*.

I have savings in the bank in England, nowhere near enough to buy a house in the UK but easily enough to buy something in Sardinia. This would be a big step. I'm single, have nothing to move back to England for and have a life style over here that I enjoy and have become accustomed to. I've been here for two years which seem to have flown by. My Italian is improving every day, I have a lot of friends and I feel like I'm starting to be part of the town. My working reputation is good and I think I'm making in-roads.

Renting is money that I'll never see again so I should at least consider buying somewhere as an investment. I can always sell it later if I need to.

Of course if I buy a house or apartment it has to be in *il centro storico*, it has to have a *terrazzo* and if possible a *camino* (the log fire is something that I've come to really cherish). I had thought of looking for something in the country, I could certainly get more for my money, but what would I do out there? I don't want to be stuck in the middle of nowhere, bored and on my own. I still want to be where the action is.

I start collecting the various property magazines that are on offer in Sassari and begin to build up a picture of what I can get for my *soldi*. I have a budget of seventy thousand pounds that converts to about ninety five thousand euros with the current exchange rate of 1.40 euros to the pound, minus various charges. I have a choice, I could buy something ready to move into or buy something that needs work, either way I can't spend more than the ninety five thousand. At first glance there seems to be a lot of property *da ristrutturare* in the historic centre and is certainly much better value in terms of square meterage. Could I really take on a dilapidated building and renovate it or is it going to be a nightmare qualifying for one of those buying a home abroad disaster programmes. I decide that a *via di mezzo* is the way forward – a place that needs work but is not out of my depth. I'm not quite sure what my depth is but confident that any major structural work is probably out of the question.

I have to calculate that the estate agent will normally take 4%, divided 50/50 between the buyer and the seller and then there will be the notary fee which is dependent on the value of the property. I need to get better informed about this as it seems to be a bit of a grey area so trot off to Tecnocasa for a bit of advice.

There are two different types of purchase tax that are combined with the Stamp Duty. The first is buying a property as a holiday home. This is 10% and is calculated on the taxable value of the property and not the purchase price (this can vary between 30% and 50% less than the purchase price). The second is the first home tax. This is 3% if the buyer purchases the property as a first home and applies for residency in the area within eighteen months (30% to 50% less than the purchase price still applies). The basic Notary fees are fixed by law and are charged according to the price of the property and range from 1- 2%.

So, the big question is whether or not I want to become a resident in Sardinia in eighteen months' time having bought a property. This would reduce the purchase tax by seven percent which is not beans. For arguments sake let's say I stay here for the next five years and the price of the property is eighty thousand. That would mean - in the worst case scenario - paying 3% of 30% less of the purchase price, 2% to the agent 2% to the notary and 750 euros that I'm told is the price of a *geometra* (surveyor). A grand total of 5,630 euros in fees. So, I calculate that for the ninety five thousand that I have I need to be looking at a place for an absolute maximum of eighty eight thousand euros if I want to buy as a first house.

Then there's the contratto or contract. An *offerta*, or offer has to be made in writing and once accepted by the seller is legally binding. If I pull out after the *offerta* is accepted I'm liable for 5% of the total property price. It is the point of no return. The next step is the *compromesso* or deposit normally between 10% and 30% and finally the *atto* which is completed in front of the *notaio* and the moment where final money and keys are exchanged.

I'm pretty confident that I have understood everything clearly but to be on the safe side will enlist the help of an Italian if I decide to go any further. Buying a house in Italy is not something you do every day and not something that you want to fuck up. We are talking about everything I have here - my savings, my capital, my life.

In the meantime I have to direct *Alice Nel Paese Delle Meraviglie* (Alice In Wonderland) for the company *La Botte e il Cilindro*. This is a serious company with a twenty-five year history of doing good quality work under the artistic directorship of Pier Paolo Conconi. They have regional and national funding and are resident at one of Sassari's three main theatres – Il Ferroviario (at the bottom of the town's main drag). It's rare that Pier Paolo gets outside *registi* in to direct shows so I feel privileged to have been given the opportunity. The acting company is a permanent ensemble most of whom I have worked with before (when they are not doing shows for *La Botte* they are encouraged to go out and work with different companies).

I only have a cast of nine but it's a cast of some of the best actors in Sassari (Ilaria Pinna, Stefania Sanna, Stefano Chessa, Luisella Conti, Nadia Imperio, Maurizio Giordo, Antonella Masala, Antonello Foddis and dancer Laura Ortu) which is just as well as there is a lot of doubling to be done. Or should I say tripling? Each actor (with the exception of Alice played by Ilaria) will have to play at least three parts. What sets this company apart from the other companies I've worked for is their ability to tour shows nationally and make sure the shows have a good run. This is a *spettacolo per Natale* (Christmas show) which will have thirty plus performances therefore standing a good chance of recouping the money it cost to stage. My other productions over here have only had two or three outings which is extremely frustrating for all that work and I don't really see the point. How can they cover the costs? Maybe they don't.

I was shocked to learn from some of the *attori* I've worked with on previous shows that most of them don't get paid for rehearsals but instead get paid by the performance. This can range from 30 euros per show to 100 euros per show. Even if you were paid the top whack and there were two performances the maximum you would walk away with is 200 euros for four weeks work. Terrible! So why do people do it? The answer is simple. If you want to act in a town that has a limited amount of theatre you accept the terms just to be able to work. People would rather perform than not. If your company can't afford to pay actors properly then you probably shouldn't be doing it. In contrast technicians get paid between 100 and 150 euros a day and will not turn up for less. Two performances plus technical rehearsals will guarantee a technician 500 euros which is non-negotiable on their part. So what makes the actor more expendable than the technician? If the actors don't turn up there is no show. If the technicians don't turn up there is no show. Incredible. The British Actors Equity Union would have something to say about that. Is there no union here? What does the elected *Assessore alla Cultura* (cultural minister) for Sassari have to say about it? (I make a point to talk to her about it). At least the actors working for *La Botte e il Cilindro* have a yearly *stipendio* which makes them the lucky ones.

Rehearsals are *divertenti* (fun) and I'm really enjoying working for this company right down to the lunches that get brought into the theatre every so often. *Pasta al forno, pollo arrosto, pane e vino* all playing their part in making it a thoroughly enjoyable *esperienza teatrale*. The show opens without any *singhiozzo* (hiccups) to a full house full of Christmas cheer. Much to my relief Pier Paolo is pleased. The last show he saw of mine was the newly named 'Shambles of the Shrew', a real bungle in the jungle that I thought might have put him off me for life. But no, *tutto bene*.

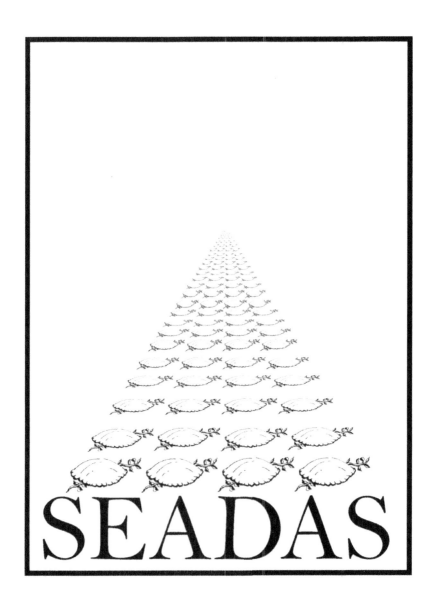

CHAPTER FOURTEEN

The New Year brings about two big changes in my life. The first is making the decision to buy a house and the second is meeting Manu (in fact that's not entirely true, I had met Manu briefly at the first night of 'Alice' and had thought at the time what a beautiful girl – an absolute stunner! Is she single?).

I'd been invited to a dinner party at Jack Evans' house by his partner Arianna Alessi (I'm not sure if they are married but either way you keep your maiden name in Italy) where I was formerly introduced to Emanuela or Manu for short. We hit it off immediately and looking back on the evening people must have thought I was really rude not wanting to talk to anyone else but her. I was smitten.

Manu was born in *Pavia* in 1977 where her parents lived at the time but both of them are originally from Sardinia. Her mother, Angela Correddu, from Villanova Monteleone (about ten kilometres south of Alghero) and her father, Giuseppe Di Biase, from La Maddalena (a small island off the north east coast of Sardegna). They now live in the small town of *Olmedo* twenty kilometres west of Sassari.

Manu graduated from the Università di Sassari with a five year, first class master's degree followed by a Postgraduate Specialization in *Chimica* (Chemistry) but told me her main passion was theatre and that she acts. I couldn't believe my luck. What are the chances of meeting somebody who has spent most of their life studying chemistry and then opts for the theatre? That's pretty special - giving up a promising, lucrative career in science for a life of poverty in the arts.

The only other thing I remember about the evening at J&A's was a very unsavoury conversation about cheese and the infamous *Casu marzu*. *Casu marzu* in Sardinian, or formaggio marcio (rotten cheese) in Italian, is a traditional Sardinian sheep milk cheese of the Pecorino variety famous for containing the live larvae of insects.

The cheese fly larvae (Piophila Casei) are deliberately introduced to the cheese prompting an advanced level of fermentation almost to the point of decomposition. The whole cheese is then left outside with part of the rind removed to allow the eggs to be laid inside. A female Piophila Casei can lay more than five hundred eggs at a time. The eggs hatch and the larvae begin to eat through the cheese with the acid from the maggots' digestive system breaking down the cheese fats. The cheese eventually becomes very soft with liquid called *lagrima*, (Latin for tear) oozing out.

The larvae are almost transparent and white in colour and grow to about 8mm long. If annoyed they can launch themselves a breath taking distance up to 15cm. Because of these athletic capabilities consumers hold their hands above the sandwich to prevent the maggots from leaping. Those who can't bear the thought of eating live maggots put the cheese in a sealed bag. Starved of oxygen the maggots squirm and jump in the bag creating a sound like rain. When the sound subsides the maggots are dead and the cheese can be eaten. Some people remove the larvae before eating the cheese but some don't. A typical Casu Marzu will contain thousands of maggots.

The cheese is considered to be unsafe to eat by some Sardinians if the maggots in the cheese have died so the cheese is consumed when the maggots are still alive.

Having made the exciting decision to buy a house I really want to get on with it and start looking for property but it'll have to wait. *Alice Nel Paese Delle Meraviglie* is playing in Cagliari for a couple of days so I take the opportunity to have a little *vacanza* and ask Manu if she wants to join me.

Apparently the region of Cagliari is famous for its production of *Zafferano* – Saffron. The farmers of San Gavino produce around sixty percent of the 'Red Gold' consumed in Italy each year. Saffron is the dried stigmas of the Crocus Sativus flower. This autumn flowering crocus is native to the Middle East, and the Phoenicians are thought to have introduced the plant to Sardinia thousands of years ago. What I didn't know is that one gram of high quality Saffron retails around the world for roughly $12 which works out at $5500 a pound. Saffron and cork are the way forward.

There are many Sardinian dishes that use Saffron including the popular southern dolce – *Pardulas* and the mouth-watering *Agnello Sardo allo zafferano.* A similar version of *Pardulas, Ricottella* is also made in the north but doesn't contain Saffron.

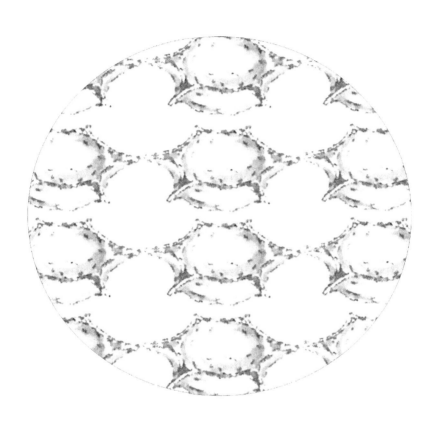

PARDULAS

Pardulas

Serves 4

Ingredients:

- *200g of semolina*
- *200g of flour*
- *500g of fresh ricotta*
- *150g of sugar*
- *50g of "strutto" (creamy pork fat)*
- *3 eggs*
- *zest of 1 lemon*
- *zest of 1 orange*
- *1 sachet of saffron (0.15 g)*
- *pinch of salt*

Preparation

Knead the semolina with the flour and diced strutto, add a pinch of salt and use some warm water to make the process easier. Keep kneading until the dough becomes compact and smooth. Shape the dough into a ball and cover with a cloth. Rest for at least 30 minutes.

Prepare the filling. In a bowl mix the fresh ricotta with the eggs, sugar, saffron, orange and lemon zest.

Roll out the dough making a thin pastry and cut out 6-8 cm diameter discs.

Once all the discs are ready (as many as can be obtained from all the dough) put one and a half tablespoons of filling on each and then lift the borders of the pastry pinching it in 5 different points (basically you need to obtain stars shapes).

Adjust the amount and shape of the filling with a spoon.

Preheat the oven to 170 degrees. Place the pardulas on a baking tray covered with greaseproof paper, brush with egg and bake for half an hour.

When ready sprinkle with castor sugar and serve.

ZAFFERANO

Agnello Sardo allo zafferano

Serves 6

Ingredients

- *1.2 kg boneless lamb*
- *1 teaspoon powdered saffron, stirred into a quarter cup of warm water*
- *small bunch of parsley, minced*
- *1/3 cup olive oil*
- *2 cloves of garlic finely chopped*
- *2/3 cup fresh tomato sauce*
- *salt and pepper*

Preparation

Chop the lamb into roughly 3cm chunks. Heat the oil in a pan and sauté the garlic and parsley. Add the lamb before the garlic turns brown and cook turning the lamb until it's sealed on all sides. Stir in the tomato and the saffron. Reduce the heat, cover, and simmer for about an hour. Add a little warm water if it looks like the meat is drying out. After about 30 minutes add seasoning to taste and serve when the meat is tender.

***

I have to be in *Cagliari* at mid-day for a technical rehearsal so we leave Sassari early in the morning giving ourselves plenty of time for the three hour trip. Heading south on the SS131 is a pretty monotonous journey. It's neither *mare* nor *montagne* and has none of the spectacular scenery that I know exists further inland. The occasional stone *Nuraghi* dotted along the roadside breaks up the monotony and gives Manu the chance to fill me in on a bit of their history.

There are some 8000 of these bee-hive like towers on the island (some of which are over twenty meters in height) only a fraction of the estimated 30,000 that used to be in existence. These pre-historic monuments can be as old as 3500 BC but to this day nobody is quite sure what they were built for. Religious temples, ordinary dwellings, rulers' residences, military strongholds, meeting halls, or a combination are all contenders. After a dozen or so of these enduring architectural enigmas we still haven't arrived.

Manu used to commute regularly between Sassari and Cagliari by train which takes five hours. You would think they would have a fast rail service between the two main cities on the island but apparently not. It doesn't even have a buffet service and you are lucky if the air conditioning works. It does however cost a paltry twelve euros for the 230 kilometre trip. You would be hard pushed to find a rail fare cheaper in Britain.

Finally, a fake *Nuraghe* signals the *zona industriale* and the out-skirts of Cagliari *città*. Thanks to Manu's expert knowledge of the town we park up quickly and find the *Piccolo Auditorium Teatro* in a matter of minutes.

We disappear into the dark interior only to emerge, blinking into the daylight, five hours later having completed the necessary rehearsal. The show starts at 9pm so plenty of time to check in to our B&B and have a little explore of *il centro storico*.

Castello, Marina, Stampace and Villanova make up the four oldest quarters of Cagliari and hold the majority of the cities bars, restaurants, hotels, museums and galleries. Our B&B called *Arcobaleno* or rainbow is located on Via Sardegna in Marina and only a stone's throw from the theatre and the bustling commercial port.

In the 1921 D.H. Lawrence book 'Sea and Sardinia' he describes Cagliari as a 'white Jerusalem without trees' referring to its barren aspect and the effect of sunlight on the limestone buildings. He also describes the city as 'strange and rather wonderful, not a bit like Italy'. Not having been to Jerusalem I can't comment on the colour but an army trees seem to have taken root since Dave Herbert's last visit almost a century ago. Far be it for me to disagree with the great man but Cagliari has become Italianized since he was last here. The cafés, bars and restaurants all sell typical Italian fare and the boutiques and shops are testament to Italy's ever growing fashion industry. I imagine that ninety years ago the topological and commercial landscape was somewhat different but today it feels distinctly part of unified Italy. It is a 'wonderful' city from what I've seen so far. The castle has amazing views of the Golfo di Cagliari and the historic centre tumbles down the hill to the water's edge. 'Strange' it is not but again I can imagine that a century ago (only forty years into unification) Sardinia was, as Lawrence described it – 'lost between Africa and Europe'.

The *Arcobaleno* turns out to be less of a hostel for Greenpeace activists and more of a chic hotel. Tastefully restored and with ensuite bathroom our *camera da letto* has an original wrought iron balcony overlooking the busy Via Sardegna and its abundant *trattorie*. Maybe not the quietest of locations but in the thick of the action and only thirty euros a night.

We make our way back to the theatre via a couple of the old town's many estate agents (I notice that the property is about a third more expensive than it is in Sassari) and then it's back into the darkness for a bit of self-styled culture. The show passes without a glitch despite the audience being a bit quieter than usual. The *Cappellaio Matto* tells me that *il pubblico* is always a little more subdued in Cagliari. Being the biggest city on the island apparently its inhabitants take themselves more seriously. But what would he know, he's only a Mad Hatter.

Immediately after the show we all head off for the obligatory congratulatory meal at a pizzeria called *I Tre Archi* (The Three Arches) on Viale Armando Diaz. It's important to remember the name and address of this shameful excuse for an eatery. I could have gone to pizza school, learnt how to make pizza, grown the ingredients, opened a restaurant, lost both arms in an accident, prepared the pizza with my feet and served it to the customer blindfolded in the time it took them to bring our food to the table. *Tripli coglioni!* - Nice building though.

The next day Manu asks me if I want to go to a vegan restaurant. You see this is what happens when you go to a bigger city – you get choice. Now you wouldn't find a vegan restaurant in Sassari and it's one of the main reasons why I live there. I suppose I'm already staying in a hotel called 'The Rainbow' and dating a chemist so adding vegan restaurants to my new found image won't do it any harm. Besides, I'm curious to know what you would eat in an Italian *ristorante vegano*.

The place is called *Terra di Mezzo,* Middle Earth, hopefully named after J.R. Tolkein's mythical 'Middle Earth' in 'The Lord of the Rings' and not the restaurant speciality.

We arrive at 9pm. I do a quick check that nobody I know is looking and cross the threshold into middle earth. It's a cosy romantic place with candles, vaulted ceilings, plenty of terracotta and a buffet style table in the middle of the room. The food turns out to be extremely tasty and costs twelve euros for as much as you can eat and this includes a free drink and water purified with reverse osmosis. As far as I understand it osmosis is the diffusion of water through a semi-permeable membrane so reversing the process would be exactly the same – wouldn't it? Now where can I find a chemist who could explain it to me? Manu!

The predominant removal mechanism in membrane filtration is straining, or size exclusion, so the process can theoretically achieve perfect exclusion of particles regardless of operational parameters such as influent pressure and concentration. Reverse Osmosis, however involves a diffusive mechanism so that separation efficiency is dependent on influent solute concentration, pressure and water flux rate. It works by using pressure to force a solution through a membrane, retaining the solute on one side and allowing the pure solvent to pass to the other side.

So, that clears that up. You see it's always useful to have your own personal chemist.

There are some vegetarian dishes on the menu. Mediterranean cuisine specialities with ethnic influences range from wholemeal pasta and wild herbs, to Middle Eastern dishes such as hummus and couscous. Typical vegan delicacies are made with tempeh, seitan and tofu.

Conversation comes easily and we talk about house prices and property in general – a favourite British pastime. In Britain buying and selling houses has become a part of our culture, the need to get on the property ladder, the need to move up and the need to make a profit. Manu explains that it's very different in Italy. Most young people live with their parents until their late twenties, early thirties when they get married and move into a home of their own. Some 70% of Italian men of the age of 29 live with their parents compared to half that number of women of the same age. It's also not at all unusual for a young couple to be given a house or apartment by the parents when they get hitched. Does this encourage lethargy? Does this mean that young Italians are less motivated as a consequence? Interestingly enough a judge at the Corte di Cassazione in 2002 turned down an appeal by a retired professor who believed that his son should fend for himself and not continue to sponge off the family. The judge ruled in favour of the 29 year old saying "There is nothing wrong in the conduct of a young person, especially if he comes from a well-to-do family, in refusing a job that does not correspond to his training, habits, attitudes and interests," The father wanted to stop a 750 euro monthly maintenance payment for his son, a law graduate, on the grounds that the lad had turned down jobs, bought a flat in a good area of town and had an investment trust worth 258,000 euros! What a precedent. Anna Oliviero Ferraris, a Rome psychology professor, said that the sentence encouraged the "pathological tendency to delay leaving the nest".

After a fifth trip back to the 'all you can eat' buffet table we pay the extremely reasonable twenty-four euros and make our way back to the *Arcobaleno* after what turned out to be a surprisingly good culinary experience.

The next day we're back in the Punto making the laborious trip back to Sassari. Why I thought the return journey might be more interesting going in the opposite direction I have no idea, but it wasn't. I would thank god for Manu's company if I was religious but settle for thanking Manu instead for coming with me.

CHAPTER FIFTEEN

I'm going to see my first *appartamento* today on Via Maddalenedda. It's on the market for seventy-seven thousand but apparently needs some work to make it habitable. The question is how much work? I arrive early for the 3pm appointment and scan the area. It's a two story corner building overlooking a small tree filled square in a relatively quiet part of the old town. The flat is on the first floor and boasts a large roof terrace as well as a *mansarda* for possible conversion. At 80 square meters in total it doesn't sound bad.

Agent Ivan arrives from Futura Immobilare on the dot of 3pm and unlocks the front door on street level. A stone staircase takes us up to the first floor landing and the master bedroom directly in front of us. Master bedroom is a bit of an overstatement as the flat only has one bedroom but plenty big enough nonetheless. Next is the living room (about the same size as the bedroom) with an adjoining door that takes us to the 'live-in' kitchen at the back of the property. From here a wooden staircase goes up to a beautiful *mansarda* and an enormous roof terrace. This is looking good. The *mansarda* would need to be converted to have a second bedroom/study but at seventy-seven thousand there would still be money to do it. I head back downstairs into the kitchen deciding that a large arch between the kitchen and living room instead of a door would open things out dramatically. The flat would benefit from being a bit more open plan giving it more space and more light. I have to say it's perfect. I don't know if I have enough money to make all the changes but it doesn't look unreasonable to me. I decide to bring Manu to have a look and also call Marco Sanna to see if he can give me a quote on the cost of the work that needs to be done. I can't believe that the first *appartamento* I've seen I'm considering buying. I don't want to rush into anything but I have a good feeling about this flat, it has great potential and is exactly what I'm looking for. Just to be on the safe side I will look at any others that come up.

Manu loves it. Despite all the work that needs to be done she insists I would be hard pushed to find a better deal. Marco arrives (I had already told him I would be moving out of his flat) and immediately starts surveying. With a little red laser gadget he carefully measures out each space in order to draw up an accurate ground plan or *planimetria*. He then proceeds to check the solidity of the floors with the highly technical manoeuvre of jumping up and down on each one. After declaring them structurally sound he asks me what work I need doing. I outline my plan for the *mansarda*, the arch and a few other bits and pieces none of which Marco thinks we can't do within my ninety-thousand euro budget. We enthusiastically shake hands and he leaves promising to come up with an accurate quote as soon as possible. *Fantastico*.

Not only does it look like I've found a *appartamento* but Manu is cooking *Risotto* tonight – with Saffron! And sun-dried tomatoes! And Sardinian Sausage!

Manu's risotto

Serves 4-5

Ingredients:

- *400-450g of short grain rice (such as arborio or carnaroli)*
- *2 sachets of saffron*
- *1 middle size onion*
- *2 spoons of extra virgin olive oil*
- *300g of fresh Sardinian sausage*
- *boiling water*
- *4-5 sundried tomatoes*
- *bunch of fresh parsley*

Preparation

Boil a kettle. Finely chop the onion and fresh parsley. Remove the sausage meat from the skin and crumble into small pieces.

Cut the sundried tomatoes into short strips.

On a low heat gently fry the chopped onion with the oil in a large non-stick pan and after two minutes add the sausage meat. Mix with the onion using a wooden spoon and sear until the sausage is brown. Keep stirring gently and add the rice. Turn the heat up, add the sundried tomatoes and stir continually while you toast the rice.

When the mixture starts to look dry add enough boiling water to cover it completely.

Keep stirring and, whenever the mixture becomes dry again, add more boiling water.

Continue until the rice is cooked al dente (generally about 10 minutes but follow the instructions on the packet) tasting continually.

When the rice is ready add the saffron and stir quickly until the colour is uniform. The risotto should be yellow and creamy.

Sprinkle with fresh parsley and serve. You can also sprinkle on fresh parmesan cheese.

Over the next week or so we see a number of other *appartamenti* but none as good as the one on Via Maddalenedda. Marco comes back with a quote of thirteen thousand for the work and as far as I'm concerned that's the green light, I'm getting close to making an offer. With impeccable timing my friend, colleague and soon to be property advisor Sally Homer comes over to stay for a few days. She agrees that the flat is a great deal and is astounded at what you can get for your money outside the exorbitantly overpriced property market in Britain. After a last consultation with Manu I decide to go for it. Sally agrees to hold my hand when I make the official offer as Manu is working and I call agent Ivan and make the appointment. Of course if I go through with the *offerta* and it is accepted I am bound by law to buy the property. If I pull out any time before the *compromeso* (the deposit) I will be liable for 5% of the property price which in this case would be 3850 euros. Not a fortune but enough to not want to lose.

I'm excited and nervous as we make our way to Futura Immobilare. This is it, once I've signed the offer there really is no going back. Ivan's waiting with the paper work when we arrive and as I skim through the pages I suddenly realize that I don't understand a word. Sally is none the wiser. This is a legal document and signing anything without fully realizing the content would be an act of complete madness. For all I know they could be selling me an olive tree. I politely ask agent Ivan if I can take the document away for an hour to let Manu have a look at it. His reluctance to let it out of his sight suddenly makes me suspicious. Maybe it is just an olive tree and a dead one at that. I'm determined and eventually leave the *ufficio* document in *mano*.

Satisfied that everything is as it should be Manu hands me back the paper work assuring me that it's not a dead *albero d'olive* and we trot off back to the *agenzia immobilare*. We arrive less than an hour after leaving. I make the offer for seventy-two thousand, five thousand below the asking price and cross my extremely sweaty fingers. I should hear by tomorrow. Congratulations ensue in true Italian style - lots of *auguri*, handshakes and *baci* etc. The whole thing took less than fifteen minutes including the kissing.

Now for a large drink. I call Manu and we head to *Gustaviños* where I order a bottle of celebratory *Prosecco* and thank Sally profusely for holding my very sweaty hand.

I'm on my way to the *stazione pullman* to put Sally on the airport bus to Alghero when my *telefonino* rings. It's agent Ivan and it's not good news. Apparently the *coglione* owner of the flat sold it to a friend two days ago. Can you fucking believe it? I muster up all the swear words I know in Italian and a few English plus a couple in French for good measure and hurl them down the telephone. Does the agent not have a contract with the owner? Obviously not! Did the owner not tell the agent two days ago? Obviously not! Am I going to be able to buy this flat? Obviously fucking not! Sally gets the gist of the conversation and looks as devastated as I feel. I hate estate agents. I'm really upset. I did everything right which is not easy in a foreign country but you can't legislate for people not doing their jobs properly. How is it possible that this can happen? The bus arrives and I have to say goodbye to Sally. It's not the sort of send off that I wanted to give her but being the philosophical trooper that she is tells me that it's my destiny to find an even better flat. Personally I think it's my destiny to do thirty years in an Italian prison for murdering an estate agent. She promises to come back soon and gets on the bus.

Manu is equally annoyed but not quite in the killing zone that I am. Against my better judgment we decide not to let it get to us as nothing is worth going to prison for. So, bloody thoughts aside, Manu reminds me that we're off to dinner in Alghero tonight with her old friends, Domenico Meloni (Melons) and Giovanna Solinas. They have promised to cook something *tipico della Sardegna* and very special. My mood lightens considerably.

Domenico is a *Ricercatore Confermato in Ispezione degli Alimenti di Origine Animale* which basically translates as food inspector. Well, more specifically, food produced by animals. Tonight they are cooking Fregola with Goat – you must be kidding!

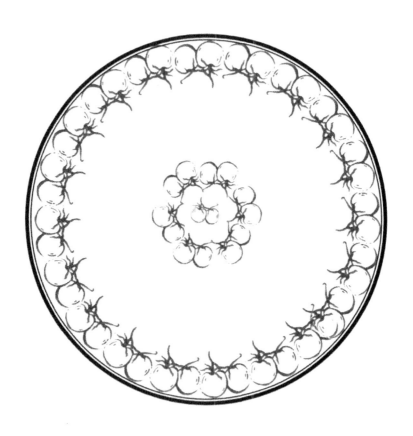

POMODORI

Fregola con Carne di Capra

Goat meat has a very strong flavour slightly like mutton but tastier. Goat is classified as red meat but is leaner and contains less cholesterol and fat than both lamb and beef. If you can't get hold of goat meat lamb will suffice. Fregola (also called fregula) is a type of pasta from Sardinia. It comes in varying sizes but typically consists of semolina dough rolled into balls 2-3 mm in diameter and toasted in an oven. This fantastic dish sounds much more appetizing in Italian than in English.

Serves 4

Ingredients

- *200g fregola*
- *350g of goat meat (or lamb)*
- *4 cups of tomato passata*
- *1 clove of garlic*
- *half an onion*
- *2-3 bay leaves (depending on taste)*
- *80g of grated pecorino cheese*
- *extra virgin olive oil*
- *salt*

Boil water for the fregola and chop the goat meat into cubes. Chop the garlic and onion and transfer into a large pan with the olive oil. Gently fry on a low heat until the onion is soft and golden. Add the chopped meat and stir until sealed (approx 5 minutes). Add the tomato passata with the bay leaves and salt. Stir and let cook for about 15 minutes.

Add the fregola and salt to the boiling water and cook until "al dente", approximately 10 minutes or less. Taste regularly to avoid over cooking (if the fregola comes from a packet you can follow the cooking time indicated).

Add the drained fregola together with some of the boiling water you have used to cook it in (as much as a small-middle sized ladle will hold) to the pan where the meat is still cooking. Let cook for a further 5 minutes.

Sprinkle with pecorino cheese and serve.

FREGOLA CON CAPRA

CHAPTER SIXTEEN

Spring comes and goes and I still haven't found an *appartamento* but have managed to stay out of *prigione*. Things are going well with Manu and we seem to spend most of our free time together. Even though she is still technically living with her parents she does have a large drawer of clothes at *casa mia*. I'm more than happy with the arrangement. Today Manu's family are coming to lunch and I do wonder if we are all going to fit into my tiny *mansarda*. At least it's only mum, dad, brother, sister and grandma and not the entire extended family which would amount to at least a couple of platoons. I've met them all before apart from Nonna Peppa (Manu's mother's mother) who turns out to be a wonderful old lady. At eighty-four years old and as tiny as a sparrow I can't help feeling a little guilty that she had to walk up the four flights of stairs. But despite her age and frame she's a bright as a button, full of energy and all dressed in black sitting in my modern *mansarda* paints quite a picture.

Born in the small village of Villanova Monteleone Nonna Peppa is the daughter of a shepherd and one of five children. By all accounts her father, Luigi Piras, was the rock of the family and community despite leading the relatively hard life of a *pastore*. Shepherds were known to go out in to the fields on a Monday with food for the week (mainly bread and cheese made by the family) and only return on a Friday to wash the only set of working clothes they had. It seems that Luigi had a little more money than most and managed to relocate the family to Alghero in the fifties and open a *panetteria* where Nonna worked for thirty years. More than sixty years on the bakery is still going strong and still belongs to the family.

Nonna and Manu's mum chat away happily in Sardo as I serve up my attempt at Italian cuisine – grilled chicken with prosciutto, melted mozzarella and basil. It seems to go down well even though I'm doubtful anyone is going to say it's rubbish. Grandma is quite a cook I'm told and I relish the invitation to go over for lunch sometime and sample her renowned *Ravioli fatti in casa*. When asked by her family what she wanted to eat on her eightieth birthday her reply was '*Un McChicken Burger da McDonalds di Alghero*'. According to *nonna* the chicken burger from McDonalds in Alghero is the tenderest chicken she has ever tasted! I clear her half-finished *piatto* and contemplate the possibility of McDonalds delivering dessert. I hear the apple pie is one of the best on the island.

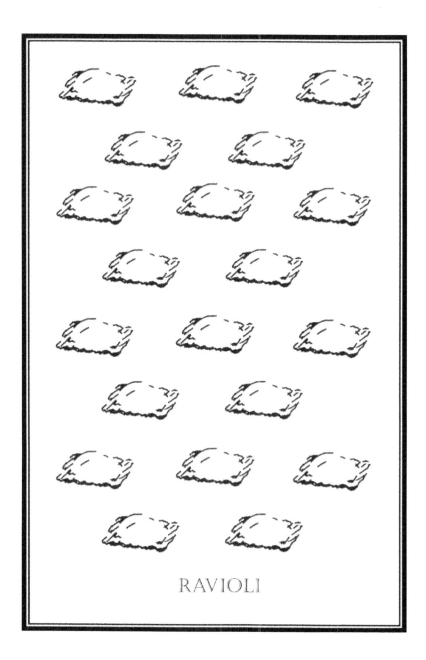

Ravioli di Nonna Peppa

This particular ravioli dish has been made by the Piras family for generations in the small town of Villanova Monteleone. 82 year old Peppa Piras (or Nonna Peppa as she is known) explains the method as passed down by her grandmother. The Ravioli can be served with butter, saffron and pecorino (or parmesan) or a simple fresh tomato sauce. Like most Italian food it is beautiful in its simplicity.

Serves 4

Ingredients

- *500g flour*
- *500g fresh ricotta (the best is in November and at Easter).*
- *100g of spinach or a bunch of parsley (Nonna Peppa prefers parsley)*
- *1 egg*
- *1/2 a teaspoon of nutmeg*
- *a few leaves of fresh mint*
- *1 lemon (zest)*
- *pinch of salt*

Preparation

Spread a little flour on a table. Put a little bit of olive oil on your hands so that the flour doesn't stick.

Mix the 500g of flour with a glass of warm water (added slowly) and work the mixture until you get a soft, elastic dough. Add a bit more water if necessary. Make the dough into a ball. Cover it with a cloth for half an hour and then start working on the ball again until the dough is smooth and soft. Divide the dough in half and using a rolling pin make two large rectangles approximately 3mm thick.

If you use spinach:

Cook the spinach for a few minutes in 1/2cm of boiling salted water. Drain getting as much water out as possible and then pat dry with kitchen towel. Finely chop the spinach (parsley if you are using it) and mint.

Mix the egg, spinach, nutmeg, lemon zest, fresh mint and salt until you have a thick paste. Take a teaspoon and put separate blobs of mixture on to the pasta rectangle at regular intervals.

Cover with the second rectangle of pasta and gently push the pasta with your fingers between one bit of ricotta and another. Separate the ravioli using a cutter or simply a small glass. Cook in boiling water for approximately 3 minutes.

PREZZEMOLO

Dressed in jeans, trainers and open shirt he doesn't appear to be one of the richest men in town but Notaio Pitzorno has reputedly made a small fortune overseeing the buying and selling of property in Sassari. He reads the *Atto* to the assembled parties including his secretary, six vendors, myself and Manu. The document is full of legal jargon but basically says that I'm buying a flat on Via San Donato 30/C, on two floors approximately ninety square meters. It has communal access on street level, a small terrace and will cost me sixty-three thousand euros excluding fees. I sign the document in five different places and proceed to write six individual checks made out to the various members of the Dalerci family for ten thousand five hundred euros each. According to the agent the six sisters inherited the property when their mother died last year and judging by the state of the apartment I'm amazed she didn't die sooner. I hand over the *assegni* and get two sets of keys in return. I've done it, I've bought a flat in Sassari.

Finally, almost two hours after arriving, we leave the *ufficio del notaio* on Viale Umberto and walk the short distance down the hill to my new *appartamento*.

It's now the beginning of November and it's taken me the best part of six months to find another property after the Via Maddalenedda fiasco and I have to concede that Sally was right - it was my destiny to find a better flat. This one is much bigger, much cheaper and has loads more potential. Including fees I've spent sixty-seven thousand which is proportionate given the amount of work that needs to be done. My only concern is that I've bitten off more that I can chew. My contempt for estate agents still lingers although my experience with Aldo from Italbeni has been a good one with no under-hand dealing and a relatively smooth transition from viewing to buying.

Via San Donato is no more than two and a half meters wide and number 30/C sits on the corner with Sassari's longest street, Via La Marmora, in the south west of the old town. Despite being so narrow Via San Donato is still a thoroughfare for traffic and even as we put the key in the lock of number 30 our arses are gently caressed by the metallic paw of a Fiat Panda wing mirror. We climb two flights of communal stairs and at last arrive at my long awaited new flat.

A pair of old *forbici* (scissors) hangs above the inside of the front door warding off unwanted evils and the smell of old age hangs in the air as a sad reminder of the former occupant. Unfortunately no *forbici* in the world could ward off the evil pine cladding that adorns the walls and ceilings and I make it my first job to thoroughly cleanse the flat of this unnatural menace.

The first floor of my new abode has a spacious hallway as you enter with steps leading up to a large living room on the right and a spare bedroom to the left. Both downstairs rooms, including the hallway, have original wooden double windows with the living room looking out on Via La Marmora and the 13th century Chiesa Di San Donato. It's a fantastic view. Another flight of stairs goes up to the kitchen with small terrace directly above the living room (also overlooking the church). A landing to the right has the bathroom sandwiched between the kitchen and master bedroom which is directly above the spare bedroom below. Everything is clad in wood apart from the floors that are all tiled. Now for the work.

Obviously *le strisce di legno* will be at the top of the list and who knows what lurks mischievously behind them. The floor tiles are either cracked or not original so will have to be replaced but this is something I will probably leave until last. The electrics and plumbing are archaic and until I have at least these two things sorted and put in a new kitchen and bathroom there's no chance of moving in. The two biggest jobs (and the ones most likely to create the most mess) are putting a fire place in the front room and expanding the terrace. The terrace is currently only two meters long by one and a half wide but by knocking down a small annex off the kitchen I can expand the terrace to just under five meters in length. The idea would then be to put a four and a half meter window separating the kitchen from the terrace giving a wonderful view of the top of the Chiesa San Donato. This doesn't come without its complications. I would have to knock down the supporting wall between the existing terrace and the kitchen and insert a massive five meter long beam to support the roof. Yikes! The *camino* in the living room is a slightly easier affair but does entail putting a hole in the kitchen floor above and running a stainless steel pipe forty centimeters in diameter up the kitchen wall and out of the roof to carry off the smoke. With the pipe visible, *a vista*, I'm hoping it will help heat the kitchen when the fire is lit below. There are a hundred and one other jobs to do but most of them I'll do *piano piano* over time. The main thing is to get it habitable as quickly as possible. The longer it takes the more I'll be paying in rent to Marco.

Manu suggests I call Jack to give me *una mano* with the basic demolition work. Jack's always looking out for a bit of extra cash between gigs and also comes with his old Peugeot estate car (that he drove over from England some fifteen years before) that will come in very handy for moving some of the debris. Good idea Manu. I give the 'Black Country Boy' (as he likes to be known despite being in his early fifties) a bell and after a bit of haggling we settle on fifty euros a day and agree to see how it goes. I tell him we'll start the following week.

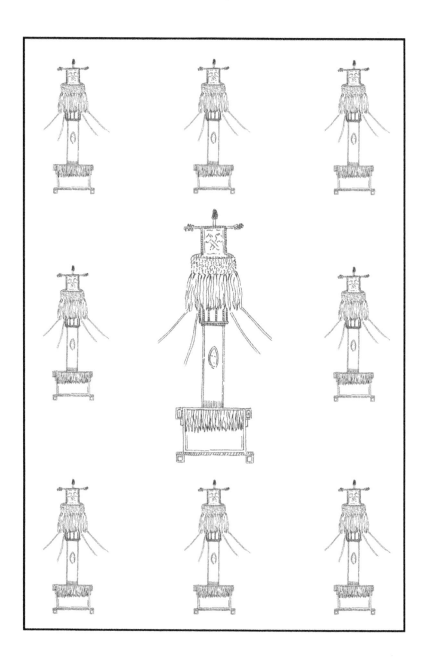

The 14th of August is *Candelieri* day – the eve of the mid-August bank holiday. The *faradda* (descent) of the *Candelieri* or the *Festha Manna*, great celebration for the Sassaresi has been celebrated for more than 700 years. Although the celebration has changed over the centuries it is still a festival in honour of the *Vergine Assunta* (Our Lady of the Assumption) and is now recognized as a UNESCO world heritage event. 200,000 people descend on the city each year to witness this amazing spectacle

Since the sixteenth century *I Candelieri* has been a religious, votive celebration in gratitude to the Virgin Mary for having freed the city of three terrible plagues, the last of which was in 1652. 90% of the population of Sassari died and the survivors who numbered a little over 5000 confirmed the votive nature of the festival, which had been votive since 1580.

Apparently all three plagues (1504, 1514 and 1652) ended on the 14th of August and this important date in the Sassaresi calendar has now become a thanksgiving.

The giant wooden candles (weighing up to 500kg) are paraded down the main drag on the shoulders of *I Gremi,* the ancient arts and crafts guilds that originated in Spain in the 16th century. There are nine *Gremi* in Sassari – the Masons, the Commercial Travelers, the Farm Workers, the Cabinet Makers, the Market Gardeners, the Cobblers, the Bricklayers, the Tailors and the Farmers. Since 1531 the farmers have been the most prestigious *Gremio*, a symbol of a city inhabited by farmers.

The traditional post *Candelieri* feast includes roast meats accompanied by the simple but delicious grilled *Melanzane alla Sasserese*.

CANDELIERI

Melanzane alla Sassarese

Ingredienti

- *4 medium aubergines*
- *½ cup extra virgin olive oil*
- *4 cloves of garlic*
- *bunch of basil*
- *salt*
- *freshly ground black pepper*

Preparation

Wash and dry the aubergines. Place them in a baking dish lightly brushed with oil and cook in a preheated oven at 180 degrees for about 30 minutes.

In the meantime peel and finely chop the garlic. Wash and dry the basil and loosely chop.

Remove the aubergines from the oven, cut them in half lengthwise and score the flesh with a sharp knife making a crisscross pattern.

In a small bowl mix the remaining oil with the basil, garlic, pinch of salt and freshly ground pepper. Drizzle over the aubergines. Arrange on a serving dish and serve hot or warm.

CHAPTER SEVENTEEN

Manu's pregnant! I'm overjoyed! I first met Manu on page 195 (that's 2 years ago in human years) and I could not think of a better way to consummate our relationship. It's been an incredible 6 years and I now feel completely at home in Sassari and have even bought an apartment that will now become a family home – *casa dolce casa*. Sardinia is a wonderful place full of characters, beautiful scenery and great food. We all have to live somewhere and Sassari is perfect for me.

The *appartamento* has ended up looking beautiful despite the myriad of problems along the way. Not least replacing the roof and its 600 tiles, replacing the rotting beams supporting the floor at a cost of five thousand euros and paying for the crane that broke lifting the 800kg beam into place to support the new roof. But with all these minor structural problems, a lot of dodgy builders (particularly one called Vittorio) and a slight bending of work permits I still managed to bring it in on budget and could almost qualify as a master builder or *Capo Cantiere* as they're called in Italy.

Simon came through and we made the film in 14 days with two weeks of rehearsal. It was a fantastic and gruelling experience shooting in the middle of the August heat with a cast and crew of 50 made up of Italians and British. Apart from the 'art' one of the highlights was the catering supplied by a company in Sassari which was absolutely superb. I say a company but it was a husband and wife team who loved to cook. They fed us all for two weeks for the incomprehensible price of 80 euros a day and to be honest it made BBC catering look like prison food. I like to think that Laura and Mario contributed to our Royal Television Society nomination for best drama! We didn't win but I don't blame them for that.

I smile at Tommaso as he orders *La staffa* and I'm brought back to the reality of the moment. '*Benvenuti nel club*' – welcome to the club he says and we toast a new chapter in my Sardinia Adventure.

Amelie Giovanna Bogdanov was born at Cliniche di San Pietro in Sassari on the 13th January 2009.

DIGESTIVO

This recipe for Limoncello is from Nonna Peppa's oldest friend 86 year old Zia Domenica.

Ingredients
- *4 organic lemons (a bit green)*
- *1 litre of 98% proof alcohol (if you can't find it you can use a good quality vodka)*
- *1kg of sugar*
- *1 litre of water*

Peel the lemons so that the zest is cut into big bits and remove any white parts remaining.

Put the zest in the alcohol for 2 days (even more is fine). After this keep the alcohol and remove the zest.

Dissolve the sugar in the water (adding a bit at a time and always stirring) and then let it boil for 3 minutes. When this mixture has cooled down add the alcohol to it.

Sieve the final mixture (you can use a funnel with a fabric napkin on top so that it goes straight in the bottle).

Ready! Keep in the freezer!

ABOUT THE AUTHOR

Malachi is an award winning Director, Writer and Producer. He has directed over seventy professional productions and has recently directed his first feature film 'The Mandrake Root', shot entirely on location in Sardinia for European Drama Network, for which he also wrote the screenplay. The Mandrake Root was nominated for a Royal Television Society Award for Best Drama. His next film, also to be shot in Sardinia is 'From Ithaca With Love – The Odyssey', a modern interpretation of Homer's classic.

With Special Thanks to

Alessandra, Angela Correddu, Anthony Aherne, Barby Crea Bbeadscreations, Bruce French, Carl Anthony Smith, Carlo Dessi & Rosanna Castangia, Corin Mellinger, Craig Painting & James Clay, David Meikle & Olga Rashkovan, Zia Domenica Carta, Domenico Meloni & Giovanna Solinas, Drew Stocker, Ffion Bogdanov, Giuseppe Di Biase, Heidi Swedberg, Iain Mackenzie, Ilaria Pinna & Ben Harrison, Jack Evans, Jacqui Findlay, Jethro & Carol Bogdanov, Jokhim & Bob Meikle, Joseph Gallagher, Kristina Landry, Lev Sarkisov, Manu Di Biase, Marco Masia & Caterina Murrutzu, Maria Elena Mura, Matt Rozier, Michael Bogdanov & Ulrike Engelbrecht-Bogdanov, Michael Jones, Michela De Luca, Mike Rogers & Sabina Netherclift, Nonna Peppa, Paola Coletto, Patsy Bogdanov, Peter Wilkinson, Robert Chatwin, Roberto Caggiari & Patrizia Carta, Sa Mandra Agriturismo, Sharon & Ronan Paterson, Rosalind Moore, Sally Homer, Simon & Kat Stone, Sue Ellis, Tony Yates.

Bar Barroccu di Angelo Piras & Donatella Sechi, Bar Coffee Break di Antonio Manus, Cantina Sociale Oliena, L'Agnata di De André, Rinnovata Taverna Bellieni di Lillo, Salumeria di Adelaide, Scuola dell'Infanzia Marta Mameli, Tramezzino Espresso.

241

Malachi Bogdanov

Printed in Great Britain
by Amazon

20262651R00144